Songs on the Road

Wandering Religious Poets in India, Tibet, and Japan

Edited by Stefan Larsson & Kristoffer af Edholm

Published by
Stockholm University Press
Stockholm University
SE-106 91 Stockholm, Sweden
www.stockholmuniversitypress.se

Supporting Agency (funding): Vetetenskapsrådet (The Swedish Research Council) and Riksbankens Jubileumsfond
Grant number: Vetetenskapsrådet, projekt, 2013-1421 (”Utanför klostrets murar”) Riksbankens Jubileumsfond, projekt, P19-0419:1 (”Frihetssånger”)

First published 2021
Cover Illustration: *A Wandering Shaivite Ascetic with his Dog*. Opaque watercolor and gold on paper. Northern India, Mughal dynasty. https://commons.wikimedia.org/wiki/File:A_wandering_Shaivite_ascetic_with_his_dog.jpg
Cover License: Public Domain
Cover designed by Christina Lenz, Stockholm University Press

Stockholm Studies in Comparative Religion (Online) ISSN: 2002-4606

ISBN (Paperback): 978-91-7635-139-0
ISBN (EPUB): 978-91-7635-137-6
ISBN (Mobi): 978-91-7635-138-3
ISBN (PDF): 978-91-7635-136-9

DOI: https://doi.org/10.16993/bbi

Suggested citation:
Larsson, S. and af Edholm, K. (eds.). 2021. *Songs on the Road: Wandering Religious Poets in India, Tibet, and Japan.* Stockholm: Stockholm University Press. DOI: https://doi.org/10.16993/bbi. License: CC-BY 4.0.

To read the free, open access version of this book online, visit https://doi.org/10.16993/bbi or scan this QR code with your mobile device.

Stockholm Studies in Comparative Religion

Stockholm Studies in Comparative Religion (SSCR) (ISSN 2002-4606) is a peer-reviewed series initiated by Åke Hultkrantz in 1961.

While its earlier emphasis lay in ethnographic-comparative approaches to religion, the series now covers a broader spectrum of the history of religions, including the philological study of discrete traditions, large-scale comparisons between different traditions as well as theoretical and methodological concerns in the study of cross-cultural religious categories such as ritual and myth.

SSCR strives to sustain and disseminate high-quality and innovative research in the form of monographs and edited volumes, preferably in English, but in exceptional cases also in the French, German-, and Scandinavian languages.

SSCR was previously included in the series Acta Universitatis Stockholmiensis (ISSN 0562-1070). A full list of publications can be found here: http://www.erg.su.se/publikationer/skriftserier/stockholm-studies-in-comparative-religion-1.38944. Volumes still in stock can be obtained through the editors.

Editorial Board

Titles in the series

36. Jackson, P. (ed.) 2016. *Horizons of Shamanism. A Triangular Approach to the History and Anthropology of Ecstatcic Techniques*. Stockholm: Stockholm University Press. DOI: https://doi.org/10.16993/bag
37. Rydving, H. & Olsson, S. 2016. *Krig och fred i vendel- och vikingatida traditioner*. Stockholm: Stockholm University Press. DOI: https://doi.org/10.16993/bah
38. Christoyannopoulos, A. & Adams M. S. (eds.) 2017. *Essays in Anarchism & Religion: Volume I*. Stockholm: Stockholm University Press. DOI: https://doi.org/10.16993/bak
39. Christoyannopoulos, A. & Adams M. S. (eds.) 2018. *Essays in Anarchism & Religion: Volume II*. Stockholm: Stockholm University Press. DOI: https://doi.org/10.16993/bas
40. Wikström af Edholm, K., Jackson Rova, P., Nordberg, A., Sundqvist, O., & Zachrisson, T. (eds.) 2019. *Myth, Materiality, and lived Religion. In Merovingian and Viking Scandinavia*. Stockholm: Stockholm University Press. DOI: https://doi.org/10.16993/bay
41. Olsson, S. 2019. *The Hostages of the Northmen: From the Viking Age to the Middle Ages*. Stockholm: Stockholm University Press. DOI: https://doi.org/10.16993/bba
42. Christoyannopoulos, A. & Adams M. S. (eds.) 2018. *Essays in Anarchism & Religion: Volume III*. Stockholm: Stockholm University Press. DOI: https://doi.org/10.16993/bas
43. Larsson, S. & af Edholm, K. (eds.) 2021. *Songs on the Road: Wandering Religious Poets in India, Tibet, and Japan*. Stockholm: Stockholm University Press. DOI: https://doi.org/10.16993/bbi

Peer Review Policies

Stockholm University Press ensures that all book publications are peer-reviewed. Each book proposal submitted to the Press will be sent to a dedicated Editorial Board of experts in the subject area. The full manuscript is reviewed by chapter or as a whole by at least two external and independent experts. A full description of Stockholm University Press' peer-review policies can be found on the website: http://www.stockholmuniversitypress.se/site/peer-review-policies/

The Editorial Board of Stockholm Studies in Comparative Religion applied single-blind review during proposal and manuscript assessment. Professor Peter Jackson Rova at the Department of Ethnology, History of Religions and Gender Studies at Stockholm University stepped down momentarily from his role in the Editorial Board during the review process of the book, to avoid a conflict of interest.

Recognition for reviewers

Stockholm University Press and the Editorial Board would like to extend a special thanks to the reviewers who contributed to the process of editing this book.

The manuscript was reviewed by:

Knut A. Jacobsen, Professor, Study of Religions, Department of Archaeology, History, Cultural Studies and Religion, University of Bergen, Norway

Ian Rutherford, Professor of Classics, University of Reading, UK. His research interests include religious travel and cultural contact in the ancient world.

Contents

Acknowledgements

The editors would like to thank the participants in the workshop "Wandering Religious Poets" held at Stockholm University in 2017, on which this book is based, Erik af Edholm for his advice in the planning of the workshop, the department of History of Religions at Stockholm University for supporting the workshop and the book, the peer reviewers, and Margot and Rune Johansson's Foundation for financial support to publish this book.

1. Introduction

Stefan Larsson & Kristoffer af Edholm

Wandering religious poets – that is to say, poets for whom wandering is a way of life and whose poetry deals with religious themes – can be found in a variety of ancient and modern cultures. In India, Tibet, and Japan the ascetic or saint who travels from place to place has been the subject of both veneration and fear for hundreds, or even thousands, of years, as is evident in poetry by and about such persons. In oral cultures in particular, wandering poets have played important roles as custodians of myths, lore, and religious traditions, and as institutors of new ones. While for some poets travelling is a dire necessity, for others the journey functions as a spiritual quest towards a transcendent goal, or a pilgrimage involving an inner journey and spiritual transformation.[1]

In their introduction to *Wandering Poets in Ancient Greek Culture* (2009), the editors Richard Hunter & Ian Rutherford provide an overview of the phenomenon of travelling poets and poetic itinerancy (from Latin *iter* 'journey, road') in ancient Hellas. The poet, singer or rhapsodist (*poiētḗs, aoidós, rhapsōidós*) may have travelled to a city to get commissions, or to partake in a poetic contest, or perform in a festival at a sanctuary;[2] he could also accompany his patron on a journey. Like its author travels across the land, so too should his poetry and the fame it gave to both poet and patron spread far and wide.[3] In the *Odyssey*, the singer is a figure worthy of respect, counted among the craftsmen

1 Coleman & Elsner 1995:6.
2 Hesiodos, *Works and Days* 654f.
3 Pindaros, *Nemean Odes* 5.1–6; West 2007:40–45, 403–404.

How to cite this book chapter:
Larsson, S. and af Edholm, K. 2021. Introduction. In: Larsson, S. and af Edholm, K. (eds.) *Songs on the Road: Wandering Religious Poets in India, Tibet, and Japan*. Pp. 1–13. Stockholm: Stockholm University Press. DOI: https://doi.org/10.16993/bbi.a.

(*dēmioergoì*) invited from abroad to do services to men.[4] Among mythical travelling poets we find Arion,[5] Thamyris,[6] and Orpheus, founder of the Orphic mysteries.

The importance given to the poet in ancient Hellenic culture is partly to be derived from this culture's Indo-European heritage, as is evident when we compare it with the ancient Celtic, Germanic, and Indo-Iranian cultures. The Celtic bard (from Proto-Celtic **bardos* 'praise-maker') was a powerful figure, patronized by kings. The *skald* had a similar status and function in Old Norse culture.[7] The Old English poem *Widsith* describes how the *scop*, corresponding to the *skald*, has travelled widely and been rewarded for his fame-spreading songs by generous patrons. Likewise, in ancient India there were itinerant bards or rhapsodes (*kuśīlava*s, *sūta*s, *māgadha*s). In the final book of Vālmīki's epic *Rāmāyaṇa*, the exiled princes Kuśa and Lava (eponyms of *kuśīlava*s) wander about among the people, reciting the epic that celebrates the *gesta* of their father, Rāma.[8]

If we turn to times closer to our own, we find that the wandering poet, and wandering in general, fascinated the German Romantics, who looked back to Classical Antiquity and the Middle Ages for inspiration. For them, wandering could represent a spiritual journey, or freedom from prosaic *Alltagsleben*.[9] We see this in the paintings of Caspar David Friedrich and Carl Gustav Carus: contemplative wanderers in sublime landscapes, which appear to mirror the wanderer's mind and soul. Some of these artworks are reminiscent of classical Chinese landscape-painting, which was influenced by Daoism and Chan Buddhism. The most powerful expression of this Romantic fascination, however, is perhaps found in Novalis' unfinished novel *Heinrich von Ofterdingen* (1799–1800), which deals with the educational journey of a medieval poet in search of a transcendental symbol: The Blue Flower. In his vision of the union of religion and

4 Homeros, *Odyssey* 17.375–390.
5 Herodotos, *Histories* 1.24; Ovidius, *Fasti* 2.79f.
6 Homeros, *Iliad* 2.591–600; Wilson 2009.
7 West 2007:ch. 1.
8 Pathak 2014:ch. 4.
9 Gish 1964; Reimers 1977.

poetry, Novalis presents the ideal poets as wandering sages, who can lead us back to a Golden Age, calling them "rare wandering men, who at times stroll through our dwellings", "untrammelled visitors, whose golden feet make no sound and whose presence involuntarily unfolds wings in everyone."[10] In Novalis' tale the function of the wandering poet's spatial journey is merely that of a catalyst for his inner, spiritual development.[11] The relationship between the outer and the inner journey is a topic we will return to numerous times in this book.

A cross-cultural study of wandering religious poets and poetry about religious wandering, which focuses on Indian, Tibetan, and Japanese traditions, has not – to our knowledge – been undertaken before. There are numerous studies of the phenomenon of pilgrimage in Hinduism, Buddhism, and other religious traditions, some of them with a cross-cultural perspective,[12] but none which focuses on the connection between itinerant lifestyles and religious poetry. Therefore, the aim of the present book, which is based on the workshop "Wandering Religious Poets" held at Stockholm University in 2017, is to highlight some aspects of the religious poet for whom wandering is a lifestyle, as well as the religious poetry which has wandering as its subject – in a variety of religious traditions, societies and different periods of time. Besides Indian, Tibetan, and Japanese, some Indo-European comparative material is included, but we have not been able to cover certain neighbouring areas, like China, where the phenomenon of wandering poets can be found as well. This book, though its scope is limited, offers a wide range of perspectives, each chapter concentrating on one or more of the following questions:

- What is the role of the wandering religious poet within a particular culture?

---

[10] Novalis, *Heinrich von Ofterdingen* part I, ch. 6, translation by Hilty 1964:94.

[11] Frykenstedt 1966:91–92.

[12] See for example Coleman & Elsner 1995; Olivelle 2007; Eck 2012; Jacobsen 2013. See also Stasik & Trynkowska 2018.

- How does the wandering poet, as traveller and outsider, relate to local communities, sacred geography, and institutionalized religion?
- In what ways is itinerancy reflected in religious poetry?
- What type or genre of poetry does the religious wanderer compose or recite and what is the purpose of the poem/song?

The chapters are loosely structured according to the geographical location of the cultures they treat, beginning in the west and moving towards the east. Thus, we start off with Peter Jackson's contribution, **Chapter 2**, which goes furthest back in time and furthest to the west on the map – connecting, in a way, this book with the previously mentioned publication *Wandering Poets in Ancient Greek Culture*. The subject of investigation is the ritual-economic and mytho-poetic prerequisites for the itinerant sage-poet in ancient Hellas and in the earliest Indo-Iranian texts. There existed a mutual dependence between ritual specialists and patronizing warrior-elites in these cultures, which is reflected in the figures of Orpheus, the Vedic Ṛbhus, and Zaraϑuštra as wandering poets and ritual specialists in search of patrons.

As Jackson writes in an earlier piece, one can speak of a basic contrast between a "civic religiosity that celebrates and seeks to consolidate an existing community", and a "sectarian religiosity that rather seeks emancipation from the civic community through voluntary ordeals of initiation and ascetism in a quest for truth, immortality, salvation, and so forth."[13] Orpheus' movement from city to city, is a feature he shared with the first philosophers, both those who wandered literally, like Xenophanes and Crates of Thebes, and those who did so metaphorically by challenging commonly held beliefs, like Socrates. The Cynics were among the earliest philosophers to extoll wandering as emancipation from civic life. Itinerancy was made easier in the Hellenic and Roman empires, thanks to the development of networks of roads and the incorporation of city-states within the huge empires. Soteriological and cosmopolitan doctrines were introduced by wandering sages and philosophers, who went beyond civic religion.[14]

---

[13] Jackson 2016:87–88.

[14] Montiglio 2000.

In India, the early ascetic groups are a good example of emancipation from the bonds of house, family, and local community.[15] It is not surprising, therefore, that Hellenes compared the ascetics they encountered in India with their own philosophers (*philósophoi, gymnosophistaí*). Early on, wandering poets contributed to the development of the Pan-Hellenic identity and traditions, such as the Trojan Cycle and the Olympic Games.[16] In India, likewise, wandering ascetics belonging to Jaina, Buddhist, Vedic-Brahmanic, and later Hindu orders have been crucial for the spread of religious traditions and texts. For example, the Buddhist ascetic poetry included in the Pali canon, such as the *Dhammapada* and the *Suttanipāta*, which is also found in Sanskrit and Gandhari. Among the ideals propagated in these texts we find that of "wandering alone like the rhinoceros", which originates in the Indian ascetic (*śramaṇa*) milieu around the mid first millennium BCE and reappears in Tibetan texts many hundreds of years later – in an environment where, we can be sure, there were no rhinoceroses.[17]

It is this type of poetry that Kristoffer af Edholm delineates in **Chapter 3**: more precisely, the ideal of the solitary wandering renouncer in early Jaina, Buddhist, and Brahmanic aphoristic verses or songs (*gāthā*s). This type of poetry reflects the practices of renunciates prior to the construction of monasteries (*vihāra*s, *maṭha*s) and the ideal of constant wandering, except during the monsoon, a practise which is still alive in India today. In these ascetic milieus, wandering is not so much a journey as a *way of life*. Voluntary and self-centred at its core, ascetic wandering is equivalent to permanently leaving society and, ideally, to do so in solitude. This reflects the wanderer's ultimate goal: individual emancipation from *saṃsāra*. Yet, many ascetics throughout history have not lived as hermits permanently, but altered between periods of solitude and periods of interactions with society and other ascetics.

---

[15] One should not speak of "civic religion" *sensu stricto*, since direct parallels to the Hellenic and Roman concepts of city-state (*polis*, *cīvitās*) and citizen are not found in ancient India.

[16] Cf. Hunter & Rutherford 2009:19–20.

[17] See Chapters 3 and 4.

Ascetic *gāthā*-poetry forbids the itinerant renouncer to engage in various crafts associated with a vagabond-lifestyle: artistic (aesthetic, ornate or enigmatic) poetry and poetry of praise, as well as medicine and divination. Instead of seeking to form a relationship with a wealthy patron to supplicate with verses in return for economic support, the wandering renouncer composes or recites his verses for himself or his peers. In other words, ascetic poetry functions as *self-instruction and encouragement* for a life on the move. One might even say that the renunciant ideal integrates, and goes beyond, the duality of patron-and-poet, since the renouncer is a kind of spiritual world-conqueror, superior to the ordinary king/patron. At the same time the renouncer takes over, in a sense, some of the traditional functions of bard or priest as "word-master" and source of spoken wisdom – in the form of ascetic poetry.

The itinerant lifestyle of Buddhist ascetics outside the monastery also forms the background of the Tibetan material analyzed by Stefan Larsson in **Chapter 4**. The very type of song (*mgur*) composed and performed by the wandering Tibetan *yogins* in the 15th and 16th centuries, which the chapter describes, is clearly akin to that of the Indian *gāthā* in Chapter 3. Both types stand closer to the simple ballad, folk-song or lyrical poem than to the artistic poem, which emphasizes the aesthetic experience, and to the magico-ritual verse or chant (*mantra*, *ṛc*, *sāman*). The eremitical lifestyle of these Tibetan hermits, outlined in a specific genre of literature called "mountain-*dharma*" (*ri chos*), is comparable with the Theravādic ideal of forest-dweller (*vanavāsin*), as a recurring ascetic reaction against institutionalized monastic religion among some South Asian monks. The 12th century *yogin* Milarepa epitomizes this ideal in Tibet and the wandering *yogins*, described in Chapter 4, contributed in making both Milarepa and his message widely known.

Larsson describes how these Tibetan charismatic *yogins* attempted to reform Buddhism in Tibet by means of composing and printing songs and hagiographies attributed to both themselves and their forebears. A type of songs called 'songs with parting instructions' was taught to monks and *yogins* who were about to embark on long journeys, often travelling alone in remote wilderness for years. Uncertain if they would ever meet again, their teacher (*lama*) sang a song containing practical instructions and advice for the wandering *yogin*. Whereas Indian renouncers were forbidden to use their poetic skills or poems as a form of livelihood, in Tibet songs could actually function as a kind of "currency" for the travelling poet.

As mentioned above, wandering can be seen as involving both an outer and an inner journey. Life on the road, as itinerant ascetic or pilgrim (from Latin *peregrīnus* 'foreign', *peregrīnātio* 'wandering around away from one's place of origin'[18]), can be seen as an expression of liminality. Patrick Olivelle (2007) writes about the religious significance of walking in India in the form of itinerant asceticism and pilgrimage, which can entail extreme toil and pain. He argues that it is the walk itself, not the destination, that is the real transformative part of pilgrimage. Although the phenomenon of pilgrimage did not exist in Vedic religion, already Vedic texts praise the toil of journeying (as ascetic practice or as part of raiding/warfare). Descriptions of *tīrtha*s ('fords'), pilgrimage-sites located at rivers, are given in the *Mahābhārata*. This text praises the visiting of pilgrimage-sites, but also includes a passage, spoken by the wise Tulādhāra, which warns against spending one's time as a pilgrim, since "all rivers are as sacred as Sarasvatī, and all mountains are sacred": the true spiritual journey takes place in the soul.[19]

The latter idea, within the later *nirguṇa-bhakti* tradition of medieval and modern India, is dealt with by Heinz Werner Wessler in **Chapter 5**. He shows that there is a long tradition within Hinduism, still alive today, of criticizing pilgrimage, as is expressed in poetry and other forms of literature. Since the deity is delocalized – *id est* not confined to a particular geographical place – some argue that there is no real need to travel there. The 16th century *bhakta* and pilgrim Mīrābāī went in all directions of space in search of Kṛṣṇa, imagining him as a wandering *yogin*, but it was in vain: Kṛṣṇa was nowhere to be found, according to poems attributed to her:

[18] Webb 1999:7.

[19] *Mahābhārata* 12.255.39.

For you [= Kṛṣṇa], I'll make myself a *yoginī*,
wandering town to town looking for you,
looking in every grove. [...]
I have still not found my indestructible Rām, my friend,
so I'll wander forest to forest, shrieking,
crying all the time.[20]

Examples of *bhakti*-poetry in the *Śaiva* tradition can be found in the Tamil *Tēvāram*, a collection of songs attributed to South Indian wandering poet-saints, later known as *nāyaṉār* ('leaders'), who lived between the 6th and 8th centuries, which reflects the journeys they undertook.[21] The sacred sites visited by these poet-saints are as much praised as is Śiva, who in his immanent form is thought to manifest himself at the sites. The commemoration of a particular location in the Tamil landscape becomes a metaphor for the experience of the deity. However, there is also the transcendent, non-localized aspect of Śiva – as expressed in this verse by Appar, which echoes the critique of pilgrimage in other Indian traditions:

Why bathe in the Ganges or the Kaveri?
Why make a pilgrimage to Kumari's cool, fragrant beach?
Why bathe in the ocean's swelling waves?
All this is in vain, if you do not think:
The Lord is everywhere.[22]

There are hundreds of sacred places spread across the Tamil land. The songs and visits of wandering poet-saints spread the fame of certain sites, which were thought to become sacred (*tiru-*) and thus attracted more visitors.[23]

Some wandering poets are best characterized as *antinomian* figures, standing outside or opposed to institutionalized forms of religious belief and behaviours. This is found in Tibetan traditions about "crazy *yogins*" related in Chapter 4, but even more so in the Buddhist Tantric poetry discussed by Per Kværne in **Chapter 6:** the *Caryāgīti* or songs composed by peripatetic poets and *yogins* towards the end of the 1st millennium CE. The songs are usually

---

20 Translation by Hawley 1998:304.
21 Cf. Peterson 1983; 1989:162f.
22 Translation by Peterson 1989:261.
23 Spencer 1970:240.

seen as exemplifying the absurd, paradoxical "twilight-speech" (*sandhābhāṣā*) that continues in the "upside-down language" (*ulaṭbāṃsī*) of the 15th century poet Kabīr.[24] Instead of trying to detect a "secret language" or undercover the meaning of the songs, Kværne argues that one should see their form as "surrealistic", conveying the idea of identity of opposites: the secular and the spiritual. Not only were many of these poet-*yogins* living on the road, they were also "wanderers" in the sense of social outsiders, Kværne writes. This is reminiscent of some Cynic philosophers, mentioned above, who voluntarily became social outsiders and adopted antinomian behaviours.[25]

The final chapter of this book, **Chapter** 7 by Lars Vargö, goes furthest east, to Japan. Here we recognize themes from Indian and Chinese cultures, next to indigenous Japanese ones. A direct, Buddhist influence from India, via China, is discernible in the hermit-sage living on a mountain or by a river, which was a highly praised ideal in Japan, just as it was India, Tibet, and China. During the latter half of the 15th century and most of the 16th century, Japan was suffering from continuous civil wars. The roads became full of monks and poets in search of more peaceful places. The unrest also had the effect that many realized the ephemeral nature of life itself, which inspired them to write poetry. Further, the urge to wander could be a quest for experiencing the beauty of nature and the need to go through religious training. To that can be added a Zen Buddhist tradition according to which the monk had to travel on foot to various temples and Zen masters in order to have his first awakening (*kenshô*) or enlightenment (*satori*) confirmed by a master. It was common for both the novice and the head priest of a temple to express their yearning for wisdom in poems. A poet who had not wandered extensively was not as respected as one who had, and a priest who did not wander between temples and spend time on his own in remote places was considered less experienced and thus less trustworthy as a

---

24 Hess 1983.

25 One can also mention the Bāuls, travelling singers from the lower ranks of Bengal society, who can be traced back at least to the 17th century and still exist today. In passionate songs they express a view of life that is opposed to institutionalized religion.

religious teacher. Wandering was facilitated during the Tokugawa period (1603–1867) due to the building of roads and places to stay at overnight, all over Japan. Among those who frequented the roads were itinerant monks, beggars who performed ceremonies for payment, and poets who travelled to meet new adepts or masters and to take part in poetic sessions.[26]

Vargö gives an account of the life of the famous 17th century poet Matsuo Bashô, who lived most of his life alone in a hut by the Sumida river, but also undertook long and arduous travels to various temples, which he recorded in his journals and poems. Bashô was influenced by Zen Buddhism.[27] Nature has always played a large role in Japanese poetry, figuring even in poems describing relations between humans or political problems. The poets translate their experiences and aspirations in terms that resemble poetry about nature. This is seen in Bashô's verses. Take, for example, the following verse (*hokku*), which was composed during a travel in 1694, the same year that the poet died. It might at first appear to be simply an expression of melancholy and Bashô's feeling of physical solitude, but Robert Aitken argues that it reflects the Zen experience of *total* solitude – autumn being the season of loneliness (*sabishisa*):

> This road!
> With no one going –
> Autumn evening
> *Kono michi ya yuku hito nashi ni aki no kure*[28]

According to David Barnhill, Bashô's journeying exemplifies "outsiderhood". It is a form of religious wayfaring, without beginning or end, and thus different from pilgrimage.[29] Bashô's journey does not go to a specific place and is not a stage or temporary break from normal life, but is a constant state, a life "on the edge

[26] Adapted from Lars Vargö's presentation for the workshop at Stockholm University in 2017.

[27] Bashô studied for Zen masters and practised *zazen*. On Zen in Bashô's poems see Aitken 1978.

[28] Translation by Aitken 1978:80.

[29] Coleman & Elsner 1995:187–188.

of death".[30] Like the Indian and Tibetan ascetics dealt with in Chapters 3 and 4, Bashô departs from home and chooses a solitary life on the road, rather than a life in the monastery.

With this general understanding, we are ready to look at the following six chapters of the book, of which the aim is to reflect some of the importance, richness, and variety of the phenomenon of itinerancy in Asian religious traditions – leading the reader along roads travelled by many, as well as along paths tread by few.

References

Aitken, Robert. 1978. *The Zen Wave: Bashô's Haiku and Zen.* New York: Weatherhill.

Barnhill, David L. 1990. "Bashô as Bat: Wayfaring and Antistructure in the Journals of Matsuo Bashô". In: *The Journal of Asian Studies* 49 (2), 274–290.

Coleman, Simon & Elsner, John. 1995. *Pilgrimage: Past and Present in the World Religions.* London: British Museum Press.

Eck, Diana. 2012. *India: A Sacred Geography.* New York: Harmony Books.

Frykenstedt, Holger. 1966. *Idé och gestalt i tysk romantik och klassicism.* Stockholm: P.A. Norstedt & Söner.

Gish, Theodore. 1964. "Wanderlust and Wanderlied: The Motif of the Wandering Hero in German Romanticism". In: *Studies in Romanticism* 3 (4), 225–239.

Hawley, John S. 1998. "Mirabai as Wife and Yogi". In: Wimbusch, V. & Valantasis, R. (eds.), *Asceticism*, Oxford: Oxford University Press, 301–319.

Hesiodos: Evelyn-White, Hugh G. 1936. *Hesiod. Homeric Hymns, Epic Cycle, Homerica: With an English Translation.* Loeb. Cambridge, Mass.: Harvard University Press.

---

30 Barnhill 1990.

Hess, Linda. 1983. "The Cow is Sucking at the Calf's Teat: Kabir's Upside-down Language". In: *History of Religions* 22 (4), 313–337.

Homeros: Murray, A. T. 1995. *Homer. The Iliad: With an English Translation*. Loeb. Cambridge, Mass.: Harvard University Press.

Murray, A. T. 1995. *Homer. The Odyssey: With an English Translation*. Revised by G. Dimock. Loeb. Cambridge, Mass.: Harvard University Press.

Hunter, Richard & Rutherford, Ian (eds.). 2009. *Wandering Poets in Ancient Greek Culture: Travel, Locality and Pan-Hellenism*. Cambridge: Cambridge University Press.

Jackson, Peter. 2016. "The Crisis of Sacrifice". In: Jackson, P. & Sjödin, A-P. (eds.), *Philosophy and the End of Sacrifice*, Sheffield: Equinox, 87–96.

Jacobsen, Knut A. 2013. *Pilgrimage in Hindu Tradition: Salvific Space*. London: Routledge.

Mahābhārata: Sukthankar, Vishnu S. *et alii*. 1933–1966. *The Mahābhārata: For the First Time Critically Edited. I–XIX*. Poona: Bhandarkar Oriental Research Institute.

Montiglio, Silvia. 2000. "Wandering Philosophers in Classical Greece". In: *The Journal of Hellenic Studies* 120, 86–105.

Novalis: Samuel, R. (ed.). 1999. *Novalis. Schriften*. Darmstadt: Wissenschaftliche Buchgesellschaft.

Hilty, Palmer. 1964. *Novalis. Henry von Ofterdingen, a Novel: Translated*. Long Grove: Waveland Press.

Olivelle, Patrick. 2007. "On the Road: The Religious Significance of Walking". In: Byrski, M K & Nowakowska, M & Wozniak, J & Jurewicz, J (eds.). *Theatrum Mirabiliorum Indiae Orientalis: A Volume to Celebrate the 70th Birthday of Professor Maria K Byrski*. Warzawa: Dom Wydawniczy Elipsa, 173–187.

Ovidius: Frazer, James G. Sir. 1996. *Ovid's Fasti: With an English Translation*. Revised by G. P. Goold. Loeb. Cambridge, Mass.: Harvard University Press.

Pathak, Shubha. 2014. *Divine Yet Human Epics: Reflections of Poetic Rulers from Ancient Greece and India*. Hellenic Studies Series 62. Washington, DC: Centre for Hellenic Studies.

Peterson, Indira V. 1983. "Lives of the Wandering Singers: Pilgrimage and Poetry in Tamil Shaivite Hagiography". In: *History of Religions* 22 (4), 338–360.

——— 1989. *Poems to Śiva: The Hymns of the Tamil Saints*. Delhi: Motilal Banarsidass.

Pindaros: Sandys, John Sir. 1937. *The Odes of Pindar: With an Introduction and an English Translation*. Loeb. Cambridge, Mass.: Harvard University Press.

Reimers, Gerd. 1977. "Vandraren – ett motiv för romantikens konstnärer". In: Reimers, G. (ed.), *Romantikens blåa blommor: Drömmen*, Stockholm: Edition Reimers, 33–47.

Spencer, George W. 1970. "The Sacred Geography of the Tamil Shaivite Hymns". In: *Numen* 17, 232–244.

Stasik, Danuta & Trynkowska, Anna (eds.). 2018. *Journeys and Travellers in Indian Literature and Art. I–II*. Warzaw: Elipsa.

Webb, Diana. 1999. *Pilgrims and Pilgrimage in the Medieval West*. London: I. B. Tauris.

West, M. L. 2007. *Indo-European Poetry and Myth*. Oxford: Oxford University Press.

Wilson, Peter. 2009. "Thamyris the Thracian: The Archetypal Wandering Poet?" In: Hunter, H. & Rutherford, I. (eds.), *Wandering Poets in Ancient Greek Culture*, Cambridge: Cambridge University Press, 46–79.

2. Itinerancy and the Afterlife

Peter Jackson Rova[31]

Abstract

The chapter proceeds from the sense of mutual dependence that existed between rudimentary warrior-elites and specialized suppliers of prestige in archaic Greek and Indo-Iranian societies. While this tension was fraught with the danger of bankruptcy and disloyalty, it also fostered new modes of antinomian religiosity. The Greek and Vedic comparanda revolve around the notion of sacrifice as a path to fame and immortality. We catch a glimpse into such elaborate notions in a Vedic myth about three idealized craftsmen, the R̥bhus, who are rewarded with immortality by the gods for their ritual services. Similar notions are linked to the mythical figure of Orpheus and the sectarian ideals of purity and abstinence among Orphics and Pythagoreans in ancient Greek society. The chapter considers how such deep-rooted ritualistic conceptions inform the frame of mind characteristic of the wandering sage, including the notion of self-care.

I

To what land shall I go to graze my cattle?
Where shall I go to graze them?

[31] Large portions of this text are also found in Jackson 2016, in which I present a similar argument from a slightly different perspective.

How to cite this book chapter:
Jackson Rova, P. 2021. Itinerancy and the Afterlife. In: Larsson, S. and af Edholm, K. (eds.) *Songs on the Road: Wandering Religious Poets in India, Tibet, and Japan*. Pp. 15–34. Stockholm: Stockholm University Press. DOI: https://doi.org/10.16993/bbi.b.

The poet of the so-called *Kamnamaēzā Hāiti* (*Yasna* 46) begins his composition in a tone of despair and isolation.[32] Zaraϑuštra, the alleged author of the hymn, is identified in younger tradition as a prophet and founder of the Mazdayasnian religion. Nevertheless, such secondary attributions should not mislead us to consider the *Hāiti* (a portion of the Old Avestan *Gāϑās*) as the unprecedented testimony of a proselyte. Despite its ellipses and idiosyncrasies, it is a hymn steeped in the poetics of fame and social eating.

The poet introduces himself to us as a wandering priest in search of a patron's support. Excluded from clan and community, he traverses a land of deceitful rulers,[33] where the only remaining hope for future success thrives on the imagery of a still unrevealed host with good intents and gifts in plenty.[34] In other words, the fact of the poet's material poverty ('having few cattle', *kamnafšuua-*[35]) does not discount him as a spiritual bringer of prosperity. He then goes on to ponder the mutual obligations of poet and patron, bound by the stipulations of a 'contract' (*miϑra-*) according to the model of a guest-host relationship.[36] He stresses the importance of exposing deceitful clients, but also points out that these are ultimately fooling themselves as they 'shall go to the bonds of deceit's captivity'. The latter theme is further emphasized in a following stanza, where the malevolent poet-priests – collectively referred to as Kavis and Karapans – are said to have 'yoked (us) with evil actions' and hence shall become 'guests in the House of Deceit forever'. This unpleasant dwelling – conceivably the infernal terminus of sinister traffickers in ritual patron-clientage – stands in stark contrast to the elsewhere attested so-called *garō dəmāna-* ('House of Laudation'), the eschatological implications of which I intend to pursue further below.

---

32 All quotes from the *Yasnas* (= *Y*) are based on the edition of the *Gāϑās* by Humbach *et alii* (1991). I shall follow their translation as long as the interpretation does not deviate from my own. Full references to all editions and translations of the *Gāϑās* that have been consulted are found in the References.

33 *Y* 46.1.

34 *Y* 46.3.

35 *Y* 46.2.

36 *Y* 46.5.

In the second half of the hymn, the poet reappears in his new status as a recognized client at the court of Vištāspa. The generous patron has become a 'truthful ally for the great offering'. Both poet and patron are said to be worthy of 'fame' (or 'to be heard', *frašrūidiiāi*[37]), but it is lastly only on account of the sacrificial 'fee' (or 'prize', *mīžda-*) – more specifically 'by means of two fertile cows' (*gāuuā azī*) – that the latter's 'higher existence' (*parāhū-*[38]) gets realized in the poet's imagination. The last stanza develops and derives its new meaning from the traditional Indo-Iranian genre of *dānastuti* ('praise of the gift'), an inserted coda through which the poet addresses his patron in praise of experienced or expected openhandedness.[39]

A mistrustful reader of the *Kamnamaēzā Hāiti* might dismiss the whole composition as an elaborate plea for ritual remuneration: a ritual performance designed to secure its inherent value by evoking the mysterious blessings of ritual. It is easy to perceive why the marketing of such a craft occasionally attracts scorn and incredulity. Immediate enthusiasm cannot be expected from those asked to give hard currency in exchange for delayed and intangible gifts of *post-mortem* elevation, let alone from those competing for the same ritual appointments. Wandering sages have thus always incurred accusations of being charlatans and malicious practitioners of magic, both in their contemporary environment and in retrospect. Hence, the Gāthic Zaraϑuštra's characterization of deceitful clients does not differ much from how his pseudo-epigraphical counterpart Zoroaster gets characterized by Plinius the Elder, namely as the inventor of monstrous impostures of magic.[40] But there is more to be drawn from this game of advanced ritual bargaining than cynical conclusions.

The precarious condition of ritual vagrancy was also an incentive for being conceptually inventive. Extending and examining the meaning of ritual exchange, and doing so in a manner persuasive enough to win a patron's liking and financial support, was the ritual professional's best insurance against destitution.

---

37 *Y* 46.13–14.

38 *Y* 46.19.

39 Humbach *et alii* 1991, I:91f.

40 *Naturalis historiae* 30.1–2.

As I shall try to demonstrate here, the poetic skills involved in fashioning a patron's lasting fame were contiguous with the ritual invention of transfigured immutability. I intend to show that this supposedly 'ritual' invention emerges both in the Greek and Indo-Iranian world out of a common tribal past, and that the new sense of self and knowledge to which it was conducive – including phenomena such as sacrificial exegesis and ascetic practices of self-control – took independent share in a process much less evasive and enigmatic than theoreticians of axiality (building on Karl Jaspers' concept of *Achsenzeit*) have so far been prone to admit.[41]

A first step towards elucidating key moments in this process is to consider the various disguises of the itinerant ritual client, both in his role of a speaking poetic subject and as an idealized projection of that same subject. The apparent realism of Zaraϑuštra's address in the *Kamnamaēzā Hāiti* can be balanced in this regard against an inherited mythical framework of itinerant ritual specialists, the best-preserved evidence of which include traditions linked to the Greek figure of Orpheus and a triad of semi-divine travelling craftsmen addressed in Vedic poetry with a cognate appellative, the R̥bhus (pl. *r̥bhávas*, sg. *r̥bhú-* < PIE *$*h_3erb^h$-*). I first turn to the more familiar example.

II

The post-classical artistic reception of Orpheus has somewhat obscured the big picture of this complex personality in Antiquity. Apart from his roles as a wonder-working minstrel and the victim of tragic love, he was also perceived by the ancients as a founder of mysteries and the author of salvific doctrines that attracted secteristic activities all over the Greek-speaking world. While a great deal of controversy exists today as to how the concepts 'Orphic' and 'Orphism' should be properly defined and delineated, there can be little doubt that Orpheus was already being conceived as a religious authority among independent purveyors of ritual (so-called Orphics [*orphikoí*] or Orpheotelests [*orpheotelestaí*]) by the late archaic period. An early witness to this emergent phenomenon is Plato.

41 Jaspers 1949.

The key passage occurs in the second book of the *Republic*,[42] wherein Socrates engages the brothers Adeimantus and Glaucon in a conversation about the true sense of 'justice' (*dikaiosýnē*). A distinction is made throughout the conversation between being truly righteous and merely appearing to be so on account of commended 'rewards and reputations' (*misthoùs dè kaì dóxas*[43]). Such rewards may also, Adeimantus contends, extend into the poetically crafted promise of a blissful afterlife. A first example concerns two legendary figures linked to Orpheus, Musaeus and Eumolpus, who are said to 'extol' (*egkōmiázō*) justice, bringing their righteous benefactors down to Hades so as to let them enjoy eternal drunkenness at a symposium, whereas the unjust are buried in mud and forced to carry water in a sieve.[44] Poetic 'praise' (*épainos*) and 'blame' (*psógos*) can be claimed here to falsely determine virtues and vices in terms of mere appearances.[45] The ensuing passage gives an early testimony to the actual experience of itinerant 'Orphics'.[46] Adeimantus complains about 'begging-priests and seers' (*agýrtai dè kaì mánteis*) who arrive at the doors of the wealthy – some even try to win whole cities over to their cause – with persuasive promises of atonement and purification through the arrangement of sacrificial feasts. Indulgence in the childish delight of their 'initiation rites' (*teletás*) is supposed to prevail after death, but those who neglect them are threatened with suffering in the afterlife. The priests and seers are said to use books by Musaeus and Orpheus from which they confusingly chant (producing 'noise', *hómados*). A denigration, no doubt, since adherence to doctrines encoded in privately acquired scriptures (as opposed to the public inscription of sacred law) was a sign of heterodoxy in Athens during this period.[47]

It is instructive to compare this deterrent account of ritual self-marketing with the explicit strategy of the *Kamnamaēzā Hāiti*: the bond of allegiance with an awarding patron is presented by the client as a warrant for an elevated existence, whereas breach

[42] *Republic* 363c–365a.
[43] *Republic* 367d.
[44] *Republic* 363c–d.
[45] *Republic* 363e.
[46] *Republic* 364b–e.
[47] Parker 1996:55.

of a contract on either side of the bargain is severely reciprocated in the afterlife. The repudiation of such activities on Plato's behalf should not divert attention from his own share in the same spiritual legacy, for it was apparently against those competing for similar claims to truth and deliverance – whether sophists, poets, or initiators into the mysteries – that he raised his case. The *agúrtai* may be accused of persuading whole cities, but what about the city that Plato envisions in the same dialogue? Is it not just another theoretical construct meant to persuade a city? A particularly telling case of Plato's Orphic inclinations, furthermore, is the Socratic account of the souls of the wise and virtuous who, purified by philosophy, arrive at beautiful abodes in the afterlife.[48] Philosophy is conceived here as a purifying way of life that secures a 'prize of contest' (*âthlon*) after death. We have here an obvious case of intersecting frameworks, the mutual implications of which enforces both the novelty and familiarity of the message: the celebratory context of athletic contest on the one hand, and the initiatory context of the mysteries on the other.

What, then, can the legendary appearance of Orpheus teach us about the conceptual heritage associated with his name? Let us begin with a comparatively late datum: a fresco from one of the houses on the Vicolo dell'anfiteatro in Pompeii.[49] Orpheus is seen seated in the middle of the image, facing the viewer. Dressed in a long, yellow garb with a blue hem – the typical outfit of a kitharode – he holds a lyre and a plectrum. Around him are seen seated or standing females, five of which are labelled as muses, and a damaged figure on a cliff in the far back probably representing Eurydice. In the foreground on the left, Heracles is seen seated on a lion-skin with his back turned against the viewer. He listens attentively to the music with his head resting on his right hand.

Clues to the narrative subtext of the scene are found in the preface to the second book of Claudianus's 'The Abduction of Proserpina' (*De raptu Proserpine*), which the poet dedicated to the Urban Prefect of Rome, Florentinus, during his time in office by the end of the 4th century CE. Despite its late date, both the content

[48] *Phaedo* 114c.

[49] Helbig 1868:893.

and context of the preface allow us to identify a series of essentials in the transmission of Orphic lore. We are told that Orpheus has for a long while refused to sing, neglecting his required task, which brings the land of Thrace into turmoil. Heifers fear the lion, mountains and woods lament his silence, but as soon as the happy news of Hercules' capturing of the man-eating mares of the Thracian king Diomedes, the 'famed ivory' (*nobile ebur*[50]) touches once more the strings of the lyre. Winds and waves are stilled, Hebrus flows more sluggishly, poplar, pine, and oak are allured by his song. A crucial detail in the description is that Orpheus performs his miraculous task in a context of heroic fame. He is encouraged to resume his art[51] in order to extol the labours of Hercules. This circumstance has immediate bearing on the final address of the preface, in which Claudianus brings his model narrative to the fore: 'So Orpheus, so I (Claudianus); so Hercules, so you (Florentinus).' It is the fortitude of Florentinus that incites Claudianus to sing, but the mutual excellence of their labours (both the poet's and the prefect's) secures fame for them both.[52] Whereas Heracles sides with Orpheus in this scene by analogy of the patronizing aristocrat, he is recurrently seen to do so in his capacity as a prototypal Eleusinian initiate. In his capacity as initiate, the patron becomes a client of the ritual specialist, who in his turn takes over the role of the patron as a spiritual supporter of his master. Ties of patron–clientage were thus not merely hierarchical in the sense that the *patronus* possesed greater material wealth than his *cliens*, but always inherently ambiguous in the sense that the *cliens* had the capacity to persuade his *patronus* that material wealth did not automatically imply spiritual wealth.[53]

---

50 *De raptu Proserpine* 16.

51 *De raptu Proserpine* 29.

52 *De raptu Proserpine* 51–52.

53 I will henceforth consider such relationships according to the familiar model of plebeians and patricians operating within systems of servitude in ancient Roman society. Ties of patron–clientage were usually hierarchical in the sense that the *patronus* possessed greater wealth than the *cliens*. The *patronus* was the benefactor of the *cliens*, who in his turn was expected to offer his services to the *patronus*. The English word 'client' – in its developed sense of someone who rather *uses* the service of a professional – can be said to reflect a relation that is always inherently reciprocal. As will become

It has sometimes been misleadingly claimed that Orpheus is a singer not of *kleós*, but of *pénthos* ('grief'). Quite on the contrary, the intangible force by which to extoll fame was not just meant to honour the living; it was also the force thought to keep them alive after death. The theme of fame is no less present in epinician poetry than in the so-called 'dirges' (*thrênoi*) composed by Pindar and Simonides alike. Furthermore, the concept of a song that mysteriously moves the world to such an extent that it beguiles death[54] seems indistinguishable from the concept of undying fame that the same poets developed in a tradition said to ensue from Orpheus, the 'father of songs' (*aoidân patêr*).[55] Although Orpheus is absent from Homeric epic, the extant traditions associated with his name in post-Homeric lore are likely to reflect an ancient melic genre that was perhaps already considered distinct from the topics of epic song by the poets of the Dark Age.[56] In its developed melic sense, as it were, a hero's *kleós* could be conceived as *áphthiton* ('undecaying') and *ásbeston* ('inextinguishable') according to the same logic of privation – that is, irresistable to forgetfulness in a poet's memorable song – as its philosophical continuator was thought to be 'uncausing forgetfulness', *alêtheia* (Doric *alátheia*).

Poets and sages in the late archaic period have been variously assumed to associate the non-local substance of all that appears

---

apparent in the following pages, the role of the ritual client may lend some of its social characteristics to the patron. In his role as initiate, the patron becomes the client of the ritual specialist, who in his turn takes over the role of the patron as a spiritual supporter of his master.

[54] Euripides, *Alcestis* 357–59.

[55] For example, Pindar's *Pythian* 4.176.

[56] In addition to the distinction between an archaic Orphic/melic and a Homeric/epic tradition, Wilson (2009:55–56) makes the following perceptive remark regarding Thamyris the Thracian, an apparent representative of Orphic ('melic') lore *avant la lettre*: 'If we ... admit the possibility that Thamyris in the *Iliad* may have presented a tradition of religious song that proferred the hope of an afterlife radically different from that implied by the *Iliad*, the passing story of his encounter with the Muses takes on a very different character. ... Like Orpheus, Thamyris was not merely a rival to the singers of Homeric poetry, or to their authority-figures in myth, be they an archetypal Homeros, or the Muses of Olympos. Early music and poetry did not form an autonomous sphere of artistic excellence and competition. Differences in music implied differences in world-view, and in particular, in religious outlook.'

and disappears with an indestructible force of mind and memory, whether stable or ever-flowing, that clearly hearkens back to the tradition of poetic praise. Simonides perhaps came closest to linking these concepts together. Firstly, in his eulogy to those who fell at Thermopylae, wherein the Spartan king Leonidas is said to have left behind an 'ever-flowing glory' (*aénaón … kléos*[57]) – an epithet of *kléos* likewise employed by Simonides' Ionian contemporary Heraclitus.[58] Secondly, by treating 'valour' (*aretḗ*) and 'inextinguishable glory' (*ásbeston kléos*) as the intangible forces by means of which the dead are brought back 'from the house of Hades' (*dômatos ex Aídeô*[59]). Finally, in an isolated fragment virtually rephrasing Heraclitus' aphorism 'a nature tends to hide' (*phýsis krýptesthai phileî*[60]): 'appearance even constrains truth' (*tò dokeîn kaì tàn alátheian biâtai*[61]). The constitutive force of nature is likewise the undying principle of truth beyond fleeting appearances.

In addition to being considered a father of songs, Orpheus was thought to embody the very principle of undying fame by virtue of his name. He was the one 'with famous name' (*onomáklytos*[62]), that is, both a provider and receiver of the gift that made him a prototype of his guild. His inert strangeness and propensity to leave and reappear, moving disruptively from city to city, was a feature that he shared with the god most strongly tied to his name and alleged country of origin: Dionysos, the veritable 'stranger within'.[63] It was also a feature that he shared with the first Greek philosophers, both the truly itinerant ones (such as Xenophanes) and those merely metaphorically 'roaming' (*plânē*) so as to challenge commonsensical wisdom (as in the case of Socrates). Their concept of immutable truth and excellence no longer served the sole purpose of ritual persuation, but had begun to gravitate towards a new sense of politics. The true philsopher of the new *polis* must

57 *PMG* 531.9.

58 *DK* B29.

59 Simonides 126 in *Lyra Graeca* II:356.

60 *DK* B123.

61 *PMG* 598.

62 Ibycus, *PMG* 306.

63 Detienne 1989:33.

begin his precarious career as a figure of ridicule. Steering beyond the hyperboles of local politics with his cosmoplitics, he is allegorized by Plato as a 'star-gazer and babbler'[64] of little apparent use to the self-indulgent citizen. A contrast is created through such an imagery between a local politics of civic pretence and a global politics of antinomian attention. However, the transgressive and subversive aspects of the latter will merely appear threatening from within the bounds of the temporary pact, whereas the travelling supplicant carries a message of otherworldly liberation.

III

Simplistic solutions to the puzzle of Orphic origins have typically consisted in taking the foreign appearance of Orpheus in ancient art and literature at face value. His appearance in myth is thus reduced to the distorted version of a real-life Thracian 'shaman', whose foreign ways earned him the reputation as seer and magician, and the salvific doctrines associated with his name to some alien substance sprung from an exotic (whether Thracian, Phrygian, or Iranian) source. Such habits of theoretical procrastination deflect attention from the inner dynamics of ritual life and mythical imagination. Greek religion owed much of its peculiarity to the symbolic vacillations between 'foreign' (*xeînos*) and 'homely' (*oikeîos*) aspects of life, between gods who arrive and those already at home. If the citizens of Athens or Thebes conceived Dionysus as the personification of a liberating force arriving from the outside, it was not because the god was an import, but because these were his inherent characteristics. He was, in Walter Otto's wording, 'the god who arrives' (*der kommende Gott*). The inherent strangeness of Orpheus would make equal sense in this regard. His exotic Thracian appearance could be perceived more loosely as a sign of eccentricity, sufficient to mark out the itinerant client's aptitude for ritual innovation. Evidence of this original ('pre-Thracian') trait can be obtained by considering the etymology of the proper name, which links the secondary appearance of Orpheus in Greek myth to a native tradition of considerable depth and consistency.

---

[64] *Republic* 488e–489a.

The Greek name is likely to have developed from an inherited Proto-Indo-European (PIE) noun (<_*h$_3$r̥b^{h}éu-_) retained in Vedic _r̥bhú-_ to denote a '(skilled) craftsman' (→'ritual specialist').[65] The complex semantics of the underlying verbal stem can be traced through its usage in Anatolian, were it expressed the quality of someone (or something) voluntarily moving between different groups: the case of a domestic animal that voluntarily 'strays' (_ḫarapta_) into another fold, thus implying the specified sense 'change herds', or of deities asked to 'ally themselves' with their human hosts in a cultic context of commensality ('Come, eat and drink! Ally yourselves with me! [_nu=mu=ššan ḫarapdumati_]'). The quality of moving between different groups (in search of a new ally) makes a feasible semantic basis of the Vedic noun _r̥bhú-_. It may originally have signified any kind of travelling professional, but, as suggested by the secondary adjectival sense 'skillful, ingenuous' (seen in Vedic _ŕ̥bhva-_, from a virtual _*h$_3$ŕ̥b^h-u̯-o-_, and _ŕ̥bhvan-_, 'the skilled one', PIE <_*h$_3$ŕ̥b^h-u̯-o-n-_), especially recalled the 'fashioning' (PIE √_*tetḱ_) skills of a carpenter.

The definite uncovering of Orpheus' pre-Greek past hinges on the identification of a proper noun _*H$_3$r̥b^{h}éu̯s_ that developed (supposedly in late-PIE) from an honorific title, 'the _*h$_3$r̥b^{h}éu̯s par excellence_', '(he) who excels in wondrous crafts', or something equivalent. Both the noun and the proper noun appear side by side in _R̥gveda_ (= _RV_), the earliest collection of ancient Indian (or Vedic) poetry, with the developed adjectival sense still attached to the noun, while Greek evidence merely leaves us with an opaque proper noun. Unlike Orpheus, however, Vedic R̥bhu does not operate alone. Rather, he is conceived as the leading member of a triad, the so-called R̥bhus (plural _r̥bhávas_), whose mythical deeds and characteristics prompted the poets of the _R̥gveda_ to contemplate and advertise the achievements of their own guild. Just like Orpheus in his capacity as the fountainhead of melic poetry, the R̥bhus are represented as prototypes of the ritual clientele. It will thus prove suggestive to examine the parallel lives of Orpheus and

[65] I am proceeding here from Michael Estell's (1999) re-opening of the case of Greek Orpheus and Vedic R̥bhu. A full account of the issue is found in Jackson 2016.

the Ṛbhus in pursuit of the real-life concerns that fostered such mythical extrapolations.

Prime events in the Ṛbhus' mythical biography are the five canonical deeds of excellence for which they became famed and attained immortality: (1) multiplying Tvaṣṭar's soma cup into four, (2) fashioning the chariot (sometimes said to belong to the Aśvins), (3) fashioning the fallow bay horses of Indra, (4) fashioning a cow (carving it up or making it to give milk), and (5) rejuvenating their parents. The following verse provides a summarizing moral of the five deeds:

> The sons of Sudhanvan [= the Ṛbhus] rose to immortality by applying themselves to their labors, ritually acting well by good ritual action.[66]

The wondrous deeds themselves suffice to suggest that the crafts of the Ṛbhus were modelled after ritual acts. In less specific terms, the three brothers are also said to 'have fashioned sacrifice' and themselves to be 'seeking fame among the immortals' (*ámartyeṣu śrava ichámānāḥ*).[67]

While the Vedic poets apparently represented the Ṛbhus as idealized members of their own guild, they were also keen to emphasize the Ṛbhus' divinely authorized promotion to permanent members of the divine community. This change of status also meant that they could appear in the roles of patrons receiving priestly praise. In so far as the Ṛbhus can be understood to impersonate ideals pertinent to any priestly lineage, we need to consider the possibility that the triad's eponymous 'change of allegiance' also echoed the ritual client's innate propensity to surrender his current patron and seek out a more beneficent ally.

There is another story hinted at in some of the hymns that appears particularly relevant. It may be referred to as the 'Story of the Ṛbhus and Agohya', but it should be kept in mind that Agohya (literally 'Unconcealable') may be just another appellation of a more familiar figure, namely the god Savitar (literally 'Impeller'). By comparing these stanzas, we may single out four

66 *RV* 3.60.3c–d.

67 *RV* 1.110.5.

significant moments in the storyline: (1) The Ṛbhus wander about in search for custody; (2) they arrive at the house of Agohya/ Savitar and enjoy his hospitality; (3) they sleep in the house of their host for either twelve days or a whole year; (4) during (or in direct adjacency to) this transitional state, they exert the force of their wondrous skills on nature.

In sudden recognition of his 'own comrades', the poet Kutsa imagines the former situation of the Ṛbhus by analogy with the present hardships of unemployed poet-priests. The theme of the distressed vagrant ('in search of [pl.] daily bread', *ābhogáyam ... ichánta*) is thus employed by the poet to fulfil his own hope for future immortalization (we noticed earlier how the poet of the *Kamnamaēzā Hāiti* recalled his former calamities on the road as a foil for his eventual rise to excellence at the court of Vištāspa):

> When, [both in East and West,] you went forth in search of your daily bread,
> as certain comrades of mine,
> o sons of Sudhanvan, after your fill of roaming
> you came to the house of Savitar the pious.[68]

The next stanza informs us that Savitar, in accordance with the impelling power inherent in his name, 'impelled [them] to immortality' (*amṛtatvám ā́suvad*). The reason for their promotion is, however, not explicitly stated. They went, it simply says, 'to make Agohya heed'. We need to consult other hymns in order to learn more about the Ṛbhus' laudable service at Aghoya's. One cryptic stanza apparently refers to something the Ṛbhus did while asleep. Another stanza seems to hint at the same event, but provides more explicit information as to what might be implied by their deeds:

> When [the Ṛbhus enjoyed the hospitality] of Agohya
> [for twelve days] sleeping (there),
> (then) they made the fields good and led the rivers;
> plants arose upon the dry land and waters upon
> the low ground.[69]

---

68 *RV* 1.110.2.

69 *RV* 1.161.12.

Through these wondrous deeds, performed during sleep, the Ṛbhus apparently prove themselves worthy of immortalization because they are already behaving like immortals.

While the details of the total message escape us, it seems clear enough that the notion of Agohya's/Savitar's residence is supposed to represent an idealization version of the good patron's house. The Ṛbhus arrive at the paradigmatic 'house of the pious' (*dāśúṣo gṛhá*-[70]), they are said to enjoy the hospitality of their host,[71] and to make him heed.[72] In the case of Agohya's house, however, the paradigmatic scenery has been refurnished to evoke that of a divine dwelling. The god is no longer imagined as a temporary guest, but as a host providing shelter for his cultic servants. Solar thematics were possibly added to the scenery in order to emphasize the fact of the Ṛbhus' imminent ascent and immortalization. By such intensified degrees of imagination, the ordinary homestead in which the priest sought refuge was always a potential domicile of cult, a virtual locus of transfiguration, and, ultimately, a stepping-stone to the celestial abode of the gods. Whenever a travelling poet-priest arrived at a new house, such enhanced means of expressing the hope for a mutually prosperous coalition between patron and client no doubt came in handy.

IV

There are obvious comparative benefits to be drawn from this Vedic excursus. Just like his namesakes in the *Ṛgveda*, Orpheus performs transfiguratively, that is, not merely by relating a topic of song, but by mysteriously moving nature on a par with a divinity: the song begins to conjure that of which it sings. An example is the fragment from Simonides,[73] according to which countless birds are said to fly over Orpheus' head and fish jump straight out of the sea *in accordance with his beautiful song* (*kalâi sỳn aoidâi*). This early testimony reflects Orpheus in a role once indistinguishable from that of the quasi-historical mystagogue. In his

70 *RV* 1.110.2.
71 *RV* 4.33.7.
72 *RV* 1.110.3.
73 *PMG* 567.

joint role of a prototypal wandering singer, inventor, and initiator, he is the ultimate Jack-of-all-trades. By tuning the cosmos to his all-embracing organon, he excels in a craft lacking in immediate gain, yet rhetorically equipped to supersede all other crafts through its power over matter and mortality. His example belongs to a narrative framework within which the promulgations of latter-day religion and rarefied autotelic art had not yet begun to develop distinctive features of their own. It is also within this framework that one must seek the eschatological foundations of the philosopher's 'way of life' (*bíos*). As we already saw, the distinctly ritual notion of a life in purity – of ending up 'purified' (*kathērámenos*) in a 'pure dwelling' (*katharà oíkēsis*)[74] – was a legacy shared between Plato and his contemporary Orpheotelests. It traces a discourse impelled by the existential concerns of ritual specialists in a distant tribal past, structured around the prize and lasting value of ritual, and ultimately designed to accommodate a life perfectly at rest in its state of being thus ritually informed.

Gāthic poetry, once again, clearly testifies to the early pertinence of such a discourse. In addition to the above-mentioned thematic of the *Kamnamaēzā Hāiti* (*Y* 46), Zaraϑuštra's eschatological intimations are centred around a fixed figure of speech that brings the theme of laudation to the fore: *garō dəmānē* (or *dəmānē garō*). The figure combines two transparent Indo-Iranian nouns (the familiar term for 'house' and a noun meaning '[song] of praise, welcome' [*gar-*]) to suggest something like 'in(to) the House of Laudation' (*-ō* and *-ē* are clearly genitive and locative markers). The song of praise was a gesture of welcome enacted in typical guest–host situations, on which cultic invocations and invitations of the gods were modelled.

An eschatological interpretation of the Gāthic *garō dəmāna-* has been endorsed by many influential Iranists. H. S. Nyberg, in his comprehensive treatise on Iranian religion from 1938, concluded that the *garō dəmāna-* was the heavenly dwelling towards which the hymns of praise ascended. He argued that it was through the mediation of Ahura Mazdā's 'thought' (*manaŋhā* [instr. sg.]) and the poet's 'songs of praise' (*garōbīš* [instr. pl.]

[74] *Phaedo* 114c.

stūtąm) that the 'sacred actions of humans' were brought up to that place.

Consider, for instance, the following stanza from the last hymn in the fourth *Gāϑā*:

> What prize Zaraϑuštra
> previously promised to his adherents,
> into that House of Laudation [did the Wise] Lord
> come as the first one.
> Through good thought these (offerings)
> are committed to You, and to Truth, with benefits.[75]

It is conceivable that the notion of the 'House of Laudation' occurred to the poet and his auditor, not just as a house *in* which praise is sung, but as a dwelling forged by the poet's song. Ahura Mazdā enters into it 'as the first one' by first being subjected to poetic praise, and it is along the same itinerary that the open-handed patron will finally receive the reward of joining his supreme lord as a guest.

Could a poetic invention such as the House of Laudation perhaps be considered an enhanced projection of the poet's present locus of performance? Was the poet in fact modelling his prospect of a happy afterlife after the solemn occasion in his master's house, imagining the patron to be sitting once again among his gods, once again becoming the subject of praise alongside his gods? Such conjectures do merit consideration in view of the hints supplied by other traditions.[76] In any case, there is ample

---

[75] *Y* 51.15.

[76] I can think of no better indicator of such a poetic strategy than the notion of Valhǫll ('the hall of fallen heroes') in Old Norse poetry, which clearly emulates the festive occasion in the guest-hall of the chief. Such events were not only popular topics of epic song – as seen, for instance, in *Beowulf* – but the typical setting of their performance. The epic strategy of the paradigmatic banquet usually marks a turning point in the storyline, but it can also function as a window on other topics of song – much in the style of the classical rhetorical figure known as *ékphrasis* – through the medium of the imaginary bard in the hall. The banquet represents an idealized image of social intercourse according to the expected standards of good food, plenty of drink, and poetic performance. For an exhaustive treatment of Valhǫll in Old Norse poetry, prose, and iconography, see Dillmann in *RGA* 35 [*s.v.* Valhǫll]).

evidence in the *Gāϑās* of a contiguous relationship between the poet's praise and the patron's happy afterlife.

Offshoots of a similar development in Greek culture likewise appear in contexts of poetic praise. But similar eschatological motives, in their proper encomiastic context of lyric poetry, are also seen to inform philosophical self-understanding. Plato, in the *Phaedrus*, evokes a region above the heavens with which true knowledge is concerned. It is a region that, *unlike* (yet still by analogy with) those 'sung by the poets' (*hymnēsé tôn poiētēs*), presents itself to the sole receptacle of the mind's eye as a colourless, formless, and intangible 'plain of truth' (*alētheía pedión*).[77] Philosophical truth-seeking is characterized here by at once interrupting and dissimulating a poet's technique for fashioning a patron's lasting fame. If the latter appeals to a ludic spirit of local self-confidence, however, the former requires the dismantling of accepted experience by directing the mind towards a solid state of true being.

The philosopher and the encomiast would seem to have little in common had it not been for the ritual legacy that so neatly ties them together. It is this deep-seated legacy that I have sought to unravel here by indicating how the predicaments of ritual professionalism gave incentive to new means of ontological reasoning. It was arguably, and ironically, among itinerant traders in ritual, decisively in need of what they persuasively sought to create, that the notion of a life at rest in deathless purity received its most pregnant formulations.

V

The area from which the Mazdayasnian religion supposedly spread – the old land known to the Greeks as Arachosia – was one of the first to witness a confluence of ascetic currents that had emerged independently in India and Greece during the mid-1st millennium BCE. Centred around itinerant sages, such as Pythagoras from Samos in the West and Gautama Buddha in the East, they mark out the first historically tangible sects and schools of philosophy to challenge the established ways of reli-

---

[77] *Phaedrus* 247c–248b.

gious life. By 'established ways' I aim broadly, on the one hand, at various forms of public worship in the Greek city-states and, on the other, the traditional ('Vedic') ritual system that thrived on the mutual commitments of priestly lineages and local warrior-elites in Indo-Aryan society. The renegotiation of such prescribed forms of ritual life would come out quite differently depending on the periods and parties involved: in some cases by causing violent uprising and civic antipathy (as exemplified by the anti-Pythagorean revolts in Magna Graeca, and public attitudes toward the so-called '*bacchanalia* sacrilege' in Rome), in others by gaining support in imperial policies (as exemplified by Aśoka's and Theodosius' decrees against animal sacrifice). Especially relevant to the understanding of this dynamic, however, is that it occurred in parallel among groups who initially would have had only vague notions about each other. Nevertheless, when Greeks became more permanently exposed to Indian culture in the settlements established by Alexander the Great and the Seleucids, they seem to have conceived the antinomian lifestyle of wandering ascetics as a sign of recognition. The terms unambiguously used in the Greek and Prakrit versions of Aśoka's edicts (3rd century BCE) to capture such circles of like-minded wanderers (Greek *diatribḗ*, Prakrit *pāsaṃḍa*) indicate social phenomena that had long been familiar to Greeks and Indians alike. So strong were the ascetics' similarities in appearance and outlook that writers from the Roman-Hellenistic period even considered Greek philosophers, such as Pythagoras and Democritus, to have come under the direct influence of the 'naked wise men' (*gymnosophistaí*) of India long before the campaigns of Alexander.

Contrary to such views, I feel confident that the ritual legacy shared between speakers of Greek and Indo-Iranian may give us sufficient cues for attributing such secondary similarities to the social forces inherently at work within these communities. It was a legacy that these speakers, in enduring unawareness of each other and their common linguistic ancestry, would have claimed as their own, but one that we are now able to retroject into the prehistoric past of Indo-European pastoral societies. Exerting its influence long after the migrations out of the Pontic-Caspian steppes, it remained a characteristic means of communication between aspiring warrior-elites and professional suppliers of ritual in archaic Greek, Iranian, and Vedic societies. If we can accept that this social formation had already developed some of its rudimentary characteristics in a long-lost tribal past, it becomes less of a bewilderment to imagine the parallel moves toward its gradual reformation.

References

Detienne, Marcel. 1989. *The Cuisine of Sacrifice Among the Greeks*. Translated by P. Wissing. Chicago: University of Chicago Press.

DK = Diels, Herman & Kranz, Walther (eds.). *Die Fragmente der Vorsokratiker*. Zürich: Weidmann, 1996 [Reprint of the 6th ed. 1951–1952].

Estell, Michael. 1999. "Orpheus and R̥bhu Revisisted". In: *Journal of Indo-European Studies*, 27 (3–4), 327–334.

Helbig, Wolfgang. 1868. *Wandgemälde der vom Vesuv verschutteten Städte Campaniens*. Leipzig: Breitkopf und Härtel.

Jackson [Rova], Peter. 2016. "The Arrival of the Clients: Technologies of Fame and the Prehistory of Orphic Eschatology". In: *Historia Religionum: An International Journal*, 8, 169–194.

Jaspers, Karl. 1949. *Vom Ursprung und Ziel der Geschichte*. Munich: R. Piper & Co. Verlag.

Lyra Graeca: Edmonds, J. M. 1924. *Lyra Graeca. II*. Harvard, Mass.: Harvard University Press.

Nyberg, H. S. 1938. *Die Religionen des alten Irans*. (Reprint 1966.) Osnabrück: Otto Zeller.

Otto, Walter. 1933. *Dionysos: Mythos und Kultus*. Frankfurt am Main: Vittorio Klostermann.

Parker, Robert. 1996. *Athenian Reiligion: A History*. Oxford: Oxford University Press.

PMG = Page, D. L. 1962. *Poetae Melici Graeci*. Oxford: Clarendon Press.

RGA = Hoops, Johannes *et alii*. 1973–2008. *Reallexikon der germanischen Altertumskunde*. Berlin and New York: Walter de Gruyter.

RV = *Ṛgveda*: van Nooten, Barend A. & Holland, Garry B. 1994. *Rig Veda: A Metrically Restored Text with an Introduction and Notes*. Cambridge, Mass.: Harvard University Press.

Geldner, Karl Friedrich. 1941. *Der Rig-Veda: Aus dem Sanskrit ins Deutsche übersetzt. I–III*. Cambridge, Mass.: Harvard University Press.

Jamison, Stephanie W. & Brereton, Joel P. 2014. *The Rigveda: The Earliest Religious Poetry of India*. Oxford: Oxford University Press.

Wilson, Peter. 2009. "Thamyris the Thracian: The Archetypal Wandering Poet?" In: Hunter, Richard & Rutherford, Ian (eds.), *Wandering Poets in Ancient Greek Culture: Travel, Locality and Pan-Hellenism*. Cambridge: Cambridge University Press, 46–79.

Y = *Yasna*: Humbach, Helmut & Elfenbein, Josef & Skjærvø, Prods O. 1991. *The Gāthās of Zarathushtra and the Other Old Avestan Texts. I: Introduction, Text and Translation; II: Commentary*. Heidelberg: Carl Winter.

Kellens, Jean & Pirart, Eric. 1988–1991. *Les textes vieil-avestiques. I: Introduction, texte et traduction; II: Répertoire, grammatiqaux et lexique; III: Commentaire*. Wiesbaden: Dr. Ludwig Reichert Verlag.

Insler, Stanley. 1975. *The Gāthās of Zarathustra*. Téhéran-Liège: Édition Bibliotèque Pahlavi.

3. 'Wander Alone Like the Rhinoceros!': The Solitary, Itinerant Renouncer in Ancient Indian Gāthā-Poetry

Kristoffer af Edholm[78]

Abstract

The ancient Indian *gāthā* – a proverbial, succinct type of single-stanza poetry, often collected in thematic sets – became a favoured form of expression among groups of ascetics from the middle to the end of the 1st millennium BCE. This poetry – contrasting with the magico-ritual chant or *mantra* of the priest and the artistic poem of the aesthete – functions as (self-)instruction for the ascetic/renouncer. Examples include *gāthā*s that exhort him to be as untiring as the Sun in its daily course, or to "wander alone like the rhinoceros". This chapter delineates the figure of the solitary, wandering renouncer in a selection of Brahmanic, Jaina, and Buddhist ascetic *gāthā*-verses from that period. Particular attention is given to the use of solar and heroic imagery for describing the ideal renouncer, and how this relates to the real-life conditions of wandering renouncers.

I. The Song of the Wanderer

The legend of Rohita and Śunaḥśepa is a narrative in mixed prose and verse (a genre known as *ākhyāna*) found in a late

[78] This chapter has benefitted from comments by Erik af Edholm and participants in the Indian Text Seminar at the Department of History of Religions, Stockholm University.

How to cite this book chapter:
af Edholm, K. 2021. 'Wander Alone Like the Rhinoceros!': The Solitary, Itinerant Renouncer in Ancient Indian Gāthā-Poetry. In: Larsson, S. and af Edholm, K. (eds.) *Songs on the Road: Wandering Religious Poets in India, Tibet, and Japan*. Pp. 35–66. Stockholm: Stockholm University Press. DOI: https://doi.org/10.16993/bbi.c.

Vedic ritual text, the *Aitareyabrāhmaṇa* (ch. 7), which is meant for recitation during the royal consecration (*rājasūya*). Versions of the legend can also be found in other texts.[79] The section of the *Aitareyabrāhmaṇa* in which this narrative is found appears to have been composed in Videha during the mid 1st millennium BCE – an area and a period connected to the rise of Buddhism and Jainism. The legend of Rohita and Śunaḥśepa includes a set of five aphoristic verses – *gāthās* – composed in the classical *anuṣṭubh-śloka*-metre. Together they form a kind of song, which, although it is untitled in Sanskrit, I will refer to as the "Song of the Wanderer"; it is rather unique in Vedic ritual literature. Before we look at how the Song of the Wanderer is best understood in context of similar thematic sets of *gāthā*-verses in early Buddhist and Jaina literature, a brief summary of the narrative of Indra and Rohita is necessary.

The story goes that there was once a king, Hariścandra, who had promised to sacrifice his only son, Rohita, to the deity (*deva*) Varuṇa. When Rohita was 'fit to bear arms' (*sāmnāhuka*), *id est* upon reaching manhood, the father decided to perform the sacrifice. Having heard the terrible news, Rohita grabbed his bow and arrows and escaped into the jungle, where he roamed about for a whole year. Meanwhile Hariścandra got sick and Rohita, hearing about his father's misfortune, decided to return home. As he came near the village, however, he was confronted by a *brāhmaṇa* – the *deva* Indra in disguise – who presented his message to Rohita in the form of a *gāthā*:

> Great is the splendour of him who has exerted himself [*śrānta-*],
> so we have heard, o Rohita!
> Wicked is he who stays among men.
> Indra is the friend of the wandering man [*carant-*].[80]

Therefore, the *brāhmaṇa* exhorted Rohita to wander (*cara*). Putting his trust in him, Rohita continued his roaming for another year in

---

79 Such as *Śāṅkhayanaśrautasūtra* 15.17–27.

80 *nānā śrāntāya śrīr astīti rohita śuśruma | pāpo nṛṣadvaro jana indra ic carataḥ sakhā ||* (*Aitareyabrāhmaṇa* 7.15.1, translation based on Olivelle 2007:175 (cf. Horsch 1966:87f.). Translations are mine, unless stated otherwise. Instead of *nṛṣadvaro* the *Śāṅkhāyanaśrautasūtra* has *niṣadvaro* 'he who sits'. Each verse is followed by the exhortation to wander (*caraiveti*).

the wilderness, away from other men. As he again approached the village, Indra appeared and told him:

Endowed with flowers are the shanks of the wanderer;
his self grows and bears fruit.
All his sins are lying down,
slain by exertion [*śrama-*] on the road.[81]

Rohita went on toiling, wandering for a third year, until Indra approached him with a new stanza:

The fortune of the sitting man sits,
that of the standing man stands,
that of the man who lies down lies down,
the fortune of the wanderer [*carata-*] wanders.[82]

A fourth year went by and Indra sang to him again, this time using the imagery of the four outcomes in the royal dice-game – Kṛta being the best outcome and Kali the worst:

Kali he becomes who is lying down,
Dvāpara he who is rising,
Tretā he who is standing erect,
Kṛta he attains who is wandering [*caran*].[83]

Rohita roamed for a fifth year, until Indra recited to him the final stanza, which presents the Sun as an ideal of endurance:

Wandering [*caran*], verily, he finds honey,
wandering he finds the sweet fruit of the cluster-fig tree.
Behold the pre-eminence of the Sun,
who never wearies of wandering![84]

---

[81] *puṣpiṇyau carato jaṅghe bhūṣṇur ātmā phalagrahiḥ* | *śere 'sya sarve pāpmānaḥ śrameṇa prapathe hatāś* || (7.15.2) *Ātmā* 'self' can also mean 'body', *pra-patha-* means 'on the (long) journey, on the wide path'.

[82] *āste bhaga āsīnasyordhvas tiṣṭhati tiṣṭhataḥ* | *śete nipadyamānasya carāti carato bhagaś* || (7.15.3)

[83] *kaliḥ śayāno bhavati saṃjihānas tu dvāparaḥ* | *uttiṣṭhaṃs tretā bhavati kṛtaṃ sampadyate caraṃś* || (7.15.4)

[84] *caran vai madhu vindati caran svādum udumbaram* | *sūryasya paśya śremāṇaṃ yo na tandrayate caraṃś* || 7.15.5. The *Śāṅkhāyanaśrautasūtra* has *śramaṇa-* 'toiling, exerting oneself' instead of *śreman-*.

With this *gāthā*, and the completion of the six years of wandering, the first section of the legend comes to an end.[85] Soon thereafter, we are told, Rohita found a substitute victim for himself, Śunaḥśepa, the son of a sylvan sage, whom he exchanged for a hundred cows.[86] Rohita returned to his father with the new sacrificial victim, which was accepted by Varuṇa. How Śunaḥśepa escaped death by means of his poetic skill is another story.

II. What is ascetic *gāthā*-poetry?

Before analyzing the Song of the Wanderer, a basic understanding of the nature of *gāthā*-poetry is a prerequisite. In his seminal work *Die vedische Gāthā- und Śloka-Literatur* (1966), Paul Horsch argues that *gāthā*-literature plays an important part in the transformation from Vedic to the early non-Vedic ascetic-renunciant (*śramaṇa*) traditions during the middle to the end of the 1st millennium BCE.[87] The *gāthā*-genre can be seen as an "alternative" literature, existing parallel to the strictly priestly one. In the earliest known Indo-Aryan poetry, the *Ṛgvedasaṃhitā*, the term *gā́thā* – which originally simply meant 'verse' or 'song' – designates a liturgical composition;[88] the same is true of its Avestan counterpart *gāϑā*.[89] In Vedic India, however, *gāthā* soon came to refer solely to non-liturgical poetry, since the term *mantra* – a formula from the Vedic hymn-collections (*Saṃhitā*s) – became synonymous with liturgical verse. It is only during the late Vedic period that one can speak of *gāthā*s as constituting a separate, non-priestly literature, which is not represented in the hymn-collections yet recognized by theologians as common lore and sparsely quoted in their

---

85 *Śāṅkhāyanaśrautasūtra* 15.19 adds a seventh year and a sixth verse, in the same style as the previous ones; the first half-line is taken from the fifth verse.

86 It is not said how Rohita managed to acquire a hundred cows; he may have captured them in a raid, as befitting a young warrior (Weller 1956:86; Falk 1984).

87 Horsch 1966:482.

88 Horsch 1966:214–215.

89 In Young Avestan the term is used mainly for referring to the five Old Avestan *Gāϑās*, the 17 hymns or *Yasna*-chapters attributed to Zaraϑuštra. The metrical characteristic of the *Gāϑās*, in contrast to the early Vedic *gāthā*, is their strophic form, each with a fixed number of verse-lines and syllables.

prosaic texts,[90] such as the *Aitareyabrāhmaṇa*'s legend of Rohita and Śunaḥśepa. Closely associated with *gāthā* is the term *śloka*,[91] which in the post-Vedic period came to designate a specific metric form – the much loved *anuṣṭubh* – regardless of its content.

From the late Vedic period onwards, *gāthā* designates a verse of the proverbial, aphoristic type, in which the focus is on content, rather than on composition. When used within a narrative och didactic text, the function of the *gāthā* is to strengthen or summarize a statement in the prose text. The *gāthā* is a single-stanza poem; a verse is complete in itself, but it often appears in the texts together with other verses on the same subject, forming thematic sets or "songs", such as the "Song of the Wanderer" or the "Rhinoceros-*sutta*" (below).

*Gāthā*s in Brahmanic,[92] Buddhist, and Jaina texts should be seen in context of the broader Indian proverbial-gnomic and didactic literature: sayings, aphorisms, maxims, and precepts originating in oral tradition. One of the subgenres of *gāthā*-literature, ascetic *gāthā*s, became a favoured form of expression among groups of renouncers during the late Vedic and early post-Vedic periods. During this time, there was considerable cultural and intellectual exchange between various ascetic groups. They all seem to have made use of some sort of un-edited, pre-Aśokan, non-sectarian, floating *corpus* of sayings, similes, ideals, poetic and narrative material, which would explain the numerous shared expressions found in post-Vedic Brahmanic, early Jaina, and Buddhist ascetic

---

90 *Śatapathabrāhmaṇa* 11.5.7.10 even mentions *gāthā* as Vedic subject of study.

91 *śloka* 'verse of praise', literally 'that which is heard'. See Horsch 1966:1, 219, 223–229, 306; Gonda 1975:405–407.

92 In the term "Brahmanic" I include both the "Vedic Brahmanic" tradition (texts from the Vedic period, *circa* 1500–500 BCE) and the "neo-Brahmanic" tradition (texts from the post-Vedic period); both (in contrast to Jainism and Buddhism) regard the Vedas as authoritative and *bráhman* (the transcendent force that animates the ritual word and action; the Absolute) as an important concept. Thus, by "Brahmanic" I do not refer to the title *brāhmaṇa* ('relating to *bráhman*'), since this title is used to describe oneself both in Brahmanic texts (often in the sense of 'priest' or as member of a hereditary class) and in early Jaina and Buddhist texts (often in the sense of 'ascetic'). Cf. McGovern 2019.

poetry.[93] The *gāthās* in the Song of the Wanderer are uniform, although they neither give the impression of being the work of a single poet, nor of being invented for the legend of Rohita and Śunaḥśepa.[94] Rather, they have sprung from the "well-spring" of ancient Indian ascetic poetry. This poetry is decidedly un-scholarly, concerning itself not with complex metaphysical theory, but with the ideal renouncer's way of life and his attitude to the world.

III. Solar and royal themes

The theme of kingship runs through much of the legend of Rohita and Śunaḥśepa and its *gāthās*. The first *gāthā* in the Song of the Wanderer promises *śrī* – the 'splendour' associated with the prospering householder and with the righteous ruler – to the man who 'exerts' himself (√*ŚRAM*), isolated from other men. And in the final stanza we have the word *śreman* 'pre-eminence, distinction', which is etymologically and semantically related to *śrī*. There is also the fourth stanza's use of imagery derived from the dice-game (which is played in the royal consecration, during which the legend of Rohita and Śunaḥśepa is recited), promising the winning throw (Kṛta) to the wanderer.

The theme of kingship is, moreover, seen in that Rohita himself is a prince or *kṣatriya* (member of the warrior aristocracy, ruler) and his guide none other than the *kṣatriya*-deity Indra, disguised as a *brāhmaṇa*. The latter term may in this case signify one who observes celibacy, since it was common among *śramaṇa*s to identify the ascetic as a *brāhmaṇa*.[95] The statement "Indra is the friend of the wanderer" (*indra ic carataḥ sakhā*) in the first *gāthās* recalls Indra as "the friend of *munis*" (*muni* 'mute, ascetic sage') in a much earlier text: *Ṛgvedasaṃhitā* 8.17.14. The name Rohita ('ruddy') is itself closely connected to kingship: in the 13th book

[93] See Charpentier 1921:43; Rau 1963; Horsch 1966:453–454; Bollée 1980; Nakamura 1983; Norman 1983:58–59, 63f., 78, 82. In the *Dhammapada* "small groups of verses, linked together by refrain, structure, or metre, clearly make small poems whose pre-existence is shown by the fact that they occur in the same form in other traditions as well." (Norman 1983:59)

[94] Horsch 1966:292.

[95] See McGovern 2019.

of the *Śaunakīyasaṃhitā* the title Rohita appears to designate a ruler ascending to power, as well as the ruddy, rising Sun, personified by the king. Verse 13.4.1 alludes to the movement of an unnamed subject, who goes to the heavenly light as Savitṛ, perhaps referring to the progression of the Sun, the king, and/or the itinerant ascetic.[96]

A common idea in Vedic, epic, and later literature, is that both the ascetic and the king possess the solar characteristics of heat (*tapas*), fiery lustre (*varcas*, *tejas*), and splendour (*śrī*). The connections between Indra, the Sun, and itinerant ascetics (*brahmacārin*, *keśin*, *muni*, *vrātya*) have been explored by Moreno Dore (2015), in addition to whose observations I wish to point to the image of the solitary wandering Sun in two more passages. First, the episode from the "Book of the Forest" in the *Mahābhārata*, in which the *deva* Dharma, in disguise of a *yakṣa* ("nature spirit"), presents riddles to the illustrious king Yudhiṣṭhira, who has gone into exile, in order to test the king's wisdom. One of the riddles goes: "What is it that travels alone, who is reborn, what is the remedy against cold, and what is the great sowing(-ground)?" Yudhiṣṭhira answers correctly:

> The Sun wanders alone [*eka- vicarati*],
> the Moon is reborn,
> fire is the remedy against cold,
> Earth is the great sowing(-ground).[97]

The dialogue continues to praise the kind of ideals found in ascetic texts.[98] Note that, as in the legend of Rohita and Śunaḥśepa, we are dealing with a royal personage in forest exile (a recurring motif in ancient Indian literature): Yudhiṣṭhira. The royal context of the *yakṣa*'s riddle is even more obvious when we understand that its origin is to be sought in the Vedic royal horse-sacrifice (*aśvamedha*). In the riddle-contest (*brahmodya*) of this grand

---

[96] Dore 2015:49.

[97] *sūrya eko vicarati candramā jāyate punaḥ* | *agnir himasya bhaiṣajyaṃ bhūmir āvapanaṃ mahat* || (*Mahābhārata* 3.297.47) Throughout this chapter references to the *Mahābhārata* is to the Critical edition (Pune), if not stated otherwise.

[98] *Mahābhārata* 3.297.53, 55, 57.

ritual the *brahmán*-priest puts his question to the *hotṛ*-priest, who provides the same answer as Yudhiṣṭhira does in the epic.[99]

The message of the Song of the Wanderer, as we have seen, is that one should seek the fortune, essence, and fruit that come from a roaming lifestyle. Rohita lives as a wanderer *temporarily*, and does this within a sacrificial context, which is typical of the Vedic ritual texts, whereas the later Brahmanic and non-Vedic *gāthās*, discussed below, express the ideal of the *permanent* wandering. Patrick Olivelle suggests that the Song of the Wanderer echoes the earlier (semi-)nomadism of Indo-Aryan tribes, who would alternate between life on the move (*yoga* 'the yoke, harnessing', war and raiding) and the peaceful, settled life (*kṣema*).[100] Roaming outside human settlement – as hunter, warrior, raider, or ascetic wanderer – was attributed greater spiritual, social, and economic value than living among men.[101] Both Olivelle and Horsch[102] have suggested that the Song of the Wanderer points forward to the ideal of wandering mendicants or ascetics. The terms used by Indra to urge Rohita to exert himself (*śrānta, śrama, śramaṇa*) derive from the verbal root (√) *ŚRAM* 'to toil, exert oneself', which is used for the disciplined life of a Vedic sacrificer during his ritual of initiation, and is found in the terms *śramaṇa* 'ascetic, mendicant' and *āśrama* 'hermitage, way of life'.

Thus, in the mentioned passages, the Sun is characterized by its solitary procession: *(vi)carati* from √*CAR*, which is used both in the sense 'to wander, go', and 'to live (in a certain way), follow a discipline'. The same root is used in the Song of the Wanderer

---

99 *sū́rya ekākī́ carati candrámā jāyate púnaḥ* | *agnír dhimásya bheṣajám̐ bhū́mir āvápanam̐ mahát* || (*Vājasaneyisam̐hitā* 23.9–10, 45–46) Similarly, but in prose, in *Taittirīyabrāhmaṇa* 3.9.5: *asau vā́ ādityá ekākī́ carati téja evā́ 'varundhe* "It is yonder Sun, indeed, that moves alone [*ekākī́* √*CAR*]. (Consequently) it is fiery energy he (= the sacrificer) thus obtains." (translation by Dumont 1948:481) And *Śatapathabrāhmaṇa* 13.2.6.10: *asau vā́ ādityá ekākī́ caraty eṣá brahmavarcasám brahmavarcasám evāsmim̐s tád dhattaḥ* "It is the Sun that walks alone [*ekākī́* √*CAR*]. This is *bráhman*-lustre; the two (priests) bestow *bráhman*-lustre on him (= the sacrificer)." Indra, identified with the Sun, is wide-striding in *Ṛgvedasam̐hitā* 10.29.4 (*Śaunakīyasam̐hitā* 20.76.4).

100 Olivelle 2007:176–177.

101 Olivelle 2007:175–176, 185.

102 Horsch 1966:88.

(*cara, carataḥ, caran*). A wandering lifestyle is attributed to various ascetic figures already in early and middle Vedic texts, but in contrast to the later ascetic *gāthā*-literature, asceticism in early Vedic texts is not connected to a specific genre of (proverbial) poetry. Instead, earlier Vedic songs about ascetics typically take the form of laudatory texts full of cryptic references and expressions. One such hymn is that of the celibate student or *brahmacārin* in the *Śaunakīyasaṃhitā*:

> The *brahmacārin* wanders [√*CAR*], stirring both worlds;
> in him the *deva*s are one-minded.
> He has firmly established earth and heaven;
> he satisfies his teacher with the heat of asceticism [*tápas-*].[103]

Interestingly, in context of the link between Rohita and Indra in the later legend, the *brahmacārin* is associated, or even identified, with Indra. This is because of the *brahmacārin*'s heroic qualities,[104] but also because Indra roams alone: in *Ṛgvedasaṃhitā* 3.30.4 we learn that Indra goes about alone (*eka* + √*CAR*), smashing obstacles. Indra is also designated as *eka* in passages which stress his heroism and strength:[105] *ekavīra* 'lone hero' is an epithet given to him.[106] In *Ṛgvedasaṃhitā* 1.165.3 the Maruts, who always appear as a group, ask Indra why he travels alone. In the *Jaiminīyabrāhmaṇa*, in the chapter on the *agnihotra*, the epithet *ekavīra* is attributed to the Sun, which in turn is identified with Indra: "He [= the Sun] is the lone hero [*eka- vīra-*], who burns/shines [*tapati*] here; he is Indra..."[107]

---

[103] *brahmacārī́ṣṇaṃś carati ródasī ubhé tásmin devā́ḥ sáṃmanaso bhavanti | sá dādhāra pṛthivī́ṃ dívaṃ ca sá ācāryàṃ tápasā piparti* || (*Śaunakīyasaṃhitā* 11.5.1, translation based on Griffith 1896:68; cf. verse 6, Dore 2015:47–48; *Ṛgvedasaṃhitā* 10.109.5).

[104] The *brahmacārin* is Indra's disciple (*Śatapathabrāhmaṇa* 11.5.4.2; *Pāraskaragṛhyasūtra* 2.2.7). The *brahmacārin*, who is Indra, has shattered the demons (*Śaunakīyasaṃhitā* 11.5.7, 16; cf. *Ṛgvedasaṃhitā* 4.12.2).

[105] *Ṛgvedasaṃhitā* 1.176.2; 8.15.3; 8.16.8; 8.90.5.

[106] *Ṛgvedasaṃhitā* 10.103.1.

[107] *sa eṣa vā eko vīro ya eṣa tapaty eṣa indra...* (*Jaiminīyabrāhmaṇa* 1.8, cf. Bodewitz's translation 1973:36–37). On Indra as the Sun see *Śatapathabrāhmaṇa* 1.6.4.18, 2.3.4.12, 3.4.2.15, 4.5.5.7, 4.5.9.4, 4.6.7.11, 8.5.3.2.

Scholars have argued that the Vedic *brahmacārin* 'he who wanders/lives with *brahman*' is a forerunner of the later renouncer.[108] Two common terms for 'renouncer', *parivrājaka* and *pravrajita*, literally mean 'he who wanders about' and 'he who goes forth (into homelessness)'.[109] Originally, renouncers would wander about constantly, except during the monsoon, as the heavy rains made travelling too difficult. The *ideal* in Brahmanic renunciant traditions was to travel alone, though it is questionable if this was actually common practise (we will return to this below). This ideal is expressed in an *anuṣṭubh-śloka* from the *Manusmṛti*, a version of which also appears in the *Mahābhārata*:

> Verily, he should always wander alone [*eka* √*CAR*],
> without any companion, in order to achieve success.
> Recognizing that success is for the solitary,
> he will not forsake (anyone) and he will not be forsaken (by anyone).[110]

Another stanza from the *Mahābhārata* comes very close:

> Verily, he should wander alone [*eka* √*CAR*] according to *dharma*,
> for in *dharma* there is no companionship.
> If he confirms to this rule absolutely,
> what can a companion do?[111]

The same ideal is found in the *Saṃnyāsopaniṣads*, a collection of later Brahmanic texts on renunciation. The *Nāradaparivrājakopaniṣad*,

---

[108] Oberlies 1997.

[109] Olivelle 1974:1.

[110] *eka eva caren nityaṃ siddhyartham asahāyavān* | *siddhim ekasya saṃpaśyan na jahāti na hīyate* || (*Manusmṛti* 6.42, translation based on Olivelle 2005:150; cf. Shiraishi 1996:103–104, 125–126). Identical to *Mahābhārata* 12.237.4cd-5b except 5a which has *ekaś carati yaḥ paśyan* "he wanders alone, who is seeing (that success comes to the solitary)" (cf. 12.237.7, 22). Similarly *Mahābhārata* 12.308.28 when Janaka says: "Free from passion, I wander/live alone, standing on the highest path" (*muktarāgaś carāmy ekaḥ pade paramake sthitaḥ*). According to 12.234.9 one should "wander alone in the forest" (*araṇye vicaraikākī*). See also 1.86.5 below, which is almost identical with the Jaina *Uttarajjhayaṇa* 15.16.

[111] *eka eva cared dharmaṃ nāsti dharme sahāyatā* | *kevalaṃ vidhim āsādya sahāyaḥ kiṃ kariṣyati* || (*Mahābhārata* 12.186.31)

for example, proclaims that "alone, indeed, shall a mendicant wander".[112] And according to the *Pañcamāśramavidhi*, a man who decides to become a skyclad ascetic must abandon absolutely everything and be prepared to be regarded as a madman by society:

> Let him wander alone [*ekākī saṃ-√CAR*] on the Earth,
> as if he were a fool, a lunatic, or a goblin.[113]

One can also mention a quote in the 11th century "Collection of Ascetic Laws" (*Yatidharmasamuccaya*) by Yādava, just to illustrate the consistency of this ideal in Brahmanic ascetic traditions from different periods in time. A verse quoted from Medhātithi, in which the ascetic is compared with the constant and unhindered movement of the Sun, echoes the ideal found in ancient texts:

> (The wandering ascetic) is seen in one place in the morning,
> in another place at noon, and in yet another at sunset.
> Like the Sun, he should remain without a home
> and free from attachment.[114]

The same text, quoting Yama:

> Totally unfettered, let him always wander alone [*ekākī vi-√CAR*],
> without a companion; for when a man
> wanders alone his path becomes smooth,
> but it thwarts him when he does not.[115]

To sum up: the notion of the Sun as a prototypical solitary wanderer, which we find in the Song of the Wanderer,[116] goes back

---

112 *eka eva … caret … ekaḥ cared bhikṣuḥ* (*Nāradaparivrājakopaniṣad* ch. 7, Olivelle 1992:215).

113 *ekākī saṃcared bhūmau bālonmattapiśācavat* || (*Pañcamāśramavidhi* verse 37cd, translation by Olivelle 2012:261)

114 *ādite 'nyatra madhyāhne anyatrāstamite ravau* | *dṛśyate tv aniketaḥ syāt sūryavatsaṅgavarjitaḥ* || (*Yatidharmasamuccaya* 9.2, translation based on Olivelle 1995:150)

115 *ekākī vicaren nityaṃ muktātmā tvasahāyakaḥ* | *ekasya hi samaḥ panthā jāyate 'nyatra jīyate* || (*Yatidharmasamuccaya* 9.19, translation based on Olivelle 1995:151)

116 The singleness of the Sun is implicit in Indra's *gāthā*; Rohita wanders about alone, and the first stanza speaks about the fault of staying with other men (*pāpo nṛṣadvaro*).

to the earlier Vedic tradition and is continued in the *Mahābhārata*. It makes its appearance in a royal context (the legend of Rohita and Śunaḥśepa told in the *rājasūya*, the riddle-contest in the *aśvamedha*, and the trial of king Yudhisthira), which is understandable when we know that the Sun is also a prototypical lone hero (*ekavīra*) and ruler. The combination of *eka* + √*CAR* 'to wander alone', which is used for the Sun in the riddle-verse, also applies to the early Vedic Indra and to the Brahmanic renouncer.

IV. The solitary Jaina hero

As we turn to the Jaina material, we find that *gāhā* (the Prakrit equivalent of *gāthā*) is typically used to designate popular verses with religious content, more seldom for the ascetic poetry found in Śvetāmbara canonical texts.[117] Although the term *gāhā* (*gāthā*) in general has been superseded by the term *sutta* (Sanskrit *sūtra*), the type of Jaina literature dealt with below is, with regard to both content and style, fully in line with the definition of ascetic *gāthā*-poetry given above.

An important text for our understanding of the early Jaina mendicant ideal is the 15th chapter of the *Uttarajjhayaṇa*, which Jarl Charpentier refers to as a "Schatzkammer altjainistischer Spruch- und Legendenpoesie".[118] It consists of sixteen stanzas on the perfect mendicant (*bhikkhu*).[119] His life is one of simplicity and harshness: he must endure heat and cold, gadflies and mosquitos;[120] he must accept any kind of tasty or tasteless food, even from the household of a low-status donor.[121] The forest, through which the mendicant fares, is filled with dangerous beasts and fearful sounds, but he shall pay no attention to any of that.[122] The 7th and 8th stanzas, listing practises that are forbidden to the Jaina

[117] Horsch 1966:218. In *Uttarajjhayaṇa* 31.13 the first book of the *Sūyagaḍa* is known as "The Sixteen Gāthās", since they form sixteen chapters of verses (except the last chapter).

[118] Charpentier 1910:62.

[119] Alsdorf 1963:115f.

[120] *Uttarajjhayaṇa* 15.4, cf. 21.18. This is very similar to verse 52 of *Khaggavisāṇasutta* (see below). Cf. *Sūyagaḍa* [1.]2.2.14–16 and *Āyāra* 6.(3.)61, 7.(7.)111, 8.(3.)1f.

[121] *Uttarajjhayaṇa* 15.12–13.

[122] *Uttarajjhayaṇa* 15.14.

mendicant, are illustrative of some of the professions associated with various types of vagabonds, perhaps practised by some (fake) ascetics: healing, divination, and so on.[123] Another "profession" which a Jaina mendicant shall not engage in is that of 'one who praises with verses',[124] meaning a laudatory poet or bard, who travels from one patron or town to another (like the Buddhist convert Vaṅgīsa below). The final verse, praising solitary (Prakrit *ega-*) itinerant mendicancy,[125] is characteristic of the sentiment of this *sutta*:

> He who does not make his living from a craft,
> who is without home and friends, having conquered his senses,
> free from everything, with minimal defilement, eating little,
> having forsaken (his) home, wandering alone [*ega-*√*CAR*] – he is a mendicant.[126]

That verse is almost identical with *Mahābhārata* 1.86.5.[127]

The following two *anuṣṭubh*-verses, from other chapters in the *Uttarajjhayaṇa*, are in the same vein:

> Verily, he should wander about alone [*ega eva* √*CAR*],
> living on allowed food, overcoming all troubles,
> in a village, town, market-place, or capital.[128]

---

[123] *Uttarajjhayaṇa* 15.7, 20.45; Zysk 1998:27f.; McGovern 2019:153–155. Similar passages are found in *Suttanipāta* 927 and *Manusmṛti* 6.50.

[124] *Uttarajjhayaṇa* 15.9. Cf. *Mahābhārata* 12.234.9 which says that the solitary ascetic should not praise anyone (*niḥstutir*).

[125] See also *Uttarajjhayaṇa* 1.16.5 and *Sūyagaḍa* [1.]4.2.1.

[126] *asippa-jīvī agīhe amitte* | *ji'indie savvao vippamukke* | *aṇu-kkasāī lahu-appa-bhakkhe* | *ceccā gihaṃ egacare sa bhikkhū* || (*Uttarajjhayaṇa* 15.16, text from Alsdorf 1963:119; cf. Tatia & Kumar 1981:90)

[127] *aśilpajīvī nagṛhaś ca nityaṃ jitendriyaḥ sarvato vipramuktaḥ* | *anokasārī laghur alpacāraś caran deśān ekacaraḥ sa bhikṣuḥ* || "He who lives off no craft, is always homeless, has conquered his senses, is entirely liberated, does not frequent houses, travels lightly on short journeys, and wanders alone [*ekacaraḥ*] through the countries – he is a mendicant [*bhikṣu-*]." (*Mahābhārata* 1.86.5)

[128] *ega eva care lāḍhe abhibhūya parīsahe* | *gāme vā nagare vāvi nigame vā rāyahāṇie* || (*Uttarajjhayaṇa* 2.9, translation based on Jacobi 1895:12). The formula *eka eva* √*CAR* in this verse is found also in the verses from *Manusmṛti* and *Nāradaparivrājakopaniṣad* quoted above.

He should sit down, alone, in a burial place,
a deserted home, or at the root of a tree,
without moving, and he should not drive away anyone.[129]

Besides the theme of solitary wandering, there is use of royal imagery in Jaina ascetic texts, akin to the that of the Vedic tradition. The *bhikkhu* is compared with royal beings like the elephant, the lion, the Sun, Sakka (Indra), and so on.[130] Like a war-elephant at the frontline crushes the enemy, so does the heroic ascetic in self-control conquer his inner foe.[131] The renouncer's solitary lifestyle (*egacariyā*)[132] is known as *jinakalpa* 'the practise of the conqueror',[133] and has its *exemplum* in the 'conqueror' (Sanskrit *jina*) Mahāvīra Vardhamāna – the title *mahāvīra* means 'great hero' – who was the most recent *tīrthaṅkara* ('ford-maker', one who re-establishes the Jaina path of liberation by crossing the river/ocean of *saṃsāra*). We read in the *Āyāra* and the *Sūyagaḍa* that when Mahāvīra 'went forth' (*pavvaie*) as a renouncer he lived alone (*ega*-√*CAR*).[134] It was only after years of solitary wandering, and after attaining supreme enlightenment in meditation, that Mahāvīra began to surround himself with disciples, though the *Sūyagaḍa* is keen to point out that his *inner* solitude was always kept intact.[135]

A passage in a later text, the *Jiṇacaritta* or 'Biography of the Heroes', based on older material, describes Mahāvīra as being, among other things, "alone like the rhinoceros" (*khaggivisāṇaṃ va ega-jae* – see the Buddhist *gāthā*s below), "effulgent like the Sun" (*sūro iva ditta-tee*), free as the bird in the air, valorous like the male elephant, and his senses drawn in like the turtle's limbs – all of them common similes in ascetic literature. This is first

[129] *susāṇe sunnagāre vā rukkhamūle va egao | akukkuo nisīejjā na ya vittāsae paraṃ ||* (*Uttarajjhayaṇa* 2.10, translation based on Jacobi 1895:12). Cf. 29.39.

[130] *Uttarajjhayaṇa* 11.16f.; cf. *Jiṇacaritta* 118 below.

[131] *Uttarajjhayaṇa* 2.6–10.

[132] *Āyāra* 6.(2.)52; cf. *Sūyagaḍa* [1.]2.2.12, 1.9.30, 1.10.23.

[133] Tatia & Kumar 1981:59–69, 78–79; Caillat 2003:37.

[134] *Āyāra* 9.(2.)11, cf. 9.(1.)6, 5.(1.)17.

[135] According to Jacobi 1895, *Sūyagaḍa* [2.]6.3 relates that the ascetic Makkhali Gōśāla criticized Mahāvīra for this, but was corrected by the Jaina Ārdraka: Mahāvīra is really always single and alone (though surrounded by followers).

stated in prose and then, in some manuscripts, summarized in two *gāhā*-verses.[136] The extreme brevity of the two *gāhā*s make them, unlike most *gāthā*s, difficult to understand without prior knowledge of what each object represents (given by the oral tradition that is reflected, we must assume, in the prose[137]):

> Vessel, shell, soul, sky, wind, and autumnal water;
> lotus-leaf, turtle, bird, rhinoceros, and *bhāruṇḍa*-bird.
>
> Elephant, bull, lion, king of mountains, and unshaken ocean;
> Moon, Sun, gold, Earth, and well-kindled fire.[138]

A corresponding enumeration in prose is found in the *Ovavāiya*, but here it refers to the mendicants at the time of Mahāvīra: they were "solitary like the rhinoceros" (*khaggi-visāṇaṃ va egajāyā*), "effulgent like the Sun" (*sūro iva ditta-teyā*), and so on.[139] In the *Sūyagaḍa*, likewise, Mahāvīra is likened to the Sun and to fire:

> Omniscient, wandering about [√*CAR*] without a home,
> crossing the river (of *saṃsāra*), wise, and of unlimited perception,
> the highest one (= Mahāvīra) glows [/becomes heated]
> like the Sun,
> and he illuminates the darkness like a brilliant fire.[140]

The image of the ascetic as glowing or becoming heated through asceticism (√*TAP*), like the Sun, can be compared with the solar qualities of the Vedic wandering ascetics.

---

136 *imesiṃ payāṇaṃ doṇṇi saṃgahaṇa-gāhāo* "Of these words there are two summarizing verses." (*Jiṇacaritta* 118) See Jacobi 1879:28–29, 63.

137 Cf. the enumeration of representative objects given in a *śloka* by sage Bodhya in *Mahābhārata* 12.171.61, which is explained in another six *śloka*s in the Bombay edition (12.178.8–13).

138 *kaṃse saṃkhe jīve gagaṇe vāū ya saraya-salile ya | pukkhara-patte kumme vihage khagge ya bhāruṃde || kuṃjara vasabhe sīhe naga-rāyā ceva sāgaram akhobhe | caṃde sūre kaṇage vasuṃdharā ceva suhuya-huyavahe ||* (*Jiṇacaritta* 118, translation based on Jacobi 1884:261)

139 *Ovavāiya* 27. The order of appearance of the similes differs from the *Jiṇacaritta*, and the mirror is added.

140 *se bhūipanne aṇieacārī | ohaṃtare dhīre aṇantacakkhū | aṇuttaraṃ tappai sūrie vā | vairoyaṇinde va tamaṃ pagāse ||* (*Sūyagaḍa* [1.]6.6, translation based on Jacobi 1895:288). Cf. *Jaiminīyabrāhmaṇa* 1.8 above. Buddha Śākyamuni too is compared with, and associated with, the Sun in early texts; see Revire 2017.

V. Pali verses on wandering alone like the rhinoceros

Finally, as we come to the early Buddhist literature, it becomes clear that *gāthā*-poetry was important to the *saṅgha* founded by Buddha Śākyamuni. The *Dhammapada* and many verses in the *Suttanipāta*, *Itivuttaka*, *Udāna*, *Theragāthā*,[141] and the *Jātaka*-stanzas, are *gāthā*-literature. Among these, the *Suttanipāta*'s *Khaggavisāṇasutta*, *Uragasutta*, and *Munisutta* (possibly identical with the *Munigāthā* referred to in the Aśoka inscription[142]) are of particular interest, since they outline the ideal renouncer. According to Upali Sramon (2011), Pali literature makes a basic distinction between *gāthā* as authoritative verse-composition, and *kāveyya* (Sanskrit *kāvya*) as mere artistic poetry, the making of poems or poetry as business. The latter is a forbidden art for the monk[143] (similar to the arts forbidden for a Jaina mendicant, as we saw above), whereas the former (*gāthā*s) need not have any poetic qualities, as they are only versified for memorisation.[144] In this context one can mention the verses attributed to Vaṅgīsa, who, prior to becoming a wandering ascetic of Śākyamuni's order, was a wandering artistic poet:

> Intoxicated with skill in the poetic art,
> formerly we wandered from village to village, from town to town.
> Then we saw the Awakened One,
> gone to the far shore beyond all (worldly conditioned) phenomena.[145]

The prevalent metre of the Pali canon is the *anuṭṭubha* (Sanskrit *anuṣṭubh*) or *siloka* (*śloka*), "which has a great deal of flexibility, and seems to be equally well adapted to aphorism, question

---

[141] Some verses in the *Theragāthās* and *Therīgāthās* are rather artistic and lyrical – the authors took over imagery and conventions of contemporary *kāvya* and secular poetry – and therefore cannot be considered ascetic *gāthā*-literature (cf. Norman 1983:75–76; Lienhard 1984a:76–77).

[142] Calcutta-Bhairat inscription (*Corpus Inscriptionum Indicarum* 1925:173); Jayawickrama 1977:31f.

[143] *Dīghanikāya* 1.125, *et cetera*.

[144] Upali Sramon 2011:21.

[145] *kāveyyamattā vicarimha pubbe gāmā gāmaṃ purā puraṃ | ath' addasāmi sambuddhaṃ sabbadhammāna pāraguṃ ||* (*Theragāthā* 1253, translation by Ireland 1997; cf. Upali Sramon 2012:25, 27).

and answer, narrative, and epic."[146] It has been argued that the anthology *Suttanipāta* is as close to the teachings of Śākyamuni himself as we can get. The following points suggest that the text is "archaic", according to Nāgapriya (2014) – and, I would add, belongs to ascetic poetry: Relative absence of formulas; (re)definition of terms from the existing socio-religious discourse, such as *brāhmaṇa*;[147] emphasis is on behaviour, rather than metaphysics (virtues and qualities of the renouncer, rather than doctrine); and relative absence of systematized teachings. Some Pali *sutta*s use refrain as "organizing principle", mainly for mnemonic reasons, but are free from repetition of systematized doctrines and enumerations typical of later texts.[148]

The ideal of solitary wandering or a solitary lifestyle (*ekacariyā*)[149] is best expressed in the *Khaggavisāṇasutta* or "Rhinoceros-*sutta*" (*Suttanipāta* 1.3 or verses 35–75), also found in Gandhari[150] and Buddhist Hybrid-Sanskrit (the *Khaḍgaviṣāṇagāthā* in the *Mahāvastu*). It has been suggested that the *Khaggavisāṇasutta* was originally an independent, and perhaps not specifically Buddhist, text.[151] The refrain encourages the renouncer to "wander alone like the rhinoceros" (*eko care khaggavisāṇakappo*)[152], a simile also taken up by the Jainas, as we saw. This agrees with other animal *exempla*: the lion wandering alone (*sīhaṃ* ... *eka*-√*CAR*)[153], or

[146] Ānandajoti 2013:17. As mentioned earlier, the *śloka*/*anuṣṭubh* is closely connected to *gāthā*-literature.

[147] McGovern 2019 argues that this should not be seen as a re-definition, since ascetics in the age of Śākyamuni had as much, or even greater, right to the title *brāhmaṇa* as priest had, for it appears that it was originally not birth but celibacy (*brahmacarya*) which could make a person a *brāhmaṇa*; the neo-Brahmanic concept of *brāhmaṇa* is not earlier than the Buddhist or Jaina concept of *brāhmaṇa*.

[148] Nāgapriya 2004; Nakamura 1987:57f. Cf. Shulman 2012:385f.

[149] *Suttanipāta* 816, 820–821.

[150] Salomon 2000:38f. It diverges from the Pali version from verse 6 onwards.

[151] Jayawickrama 1977:31; Salomon 2000:14–19.

[152] *khaggavisāṇakappo* can also be translated 'following the habit/manner (Sanskrit *kalpa*) of the rhinoceros' (Caillat 2003:38). It is debated among scholars how one should translate the refrain (see Jayawickrama 1977:22–23; Wright 2001:3; Jones 2014; differently Norman 1996).

[153] *Suttanipāta* 72, 166, 416.

the solitary (senior male) elephant who has left the herd.[154] The lion and the elephant are connected to royal and heroic imagery, as in this stanza from the *Dhammapada*: if one does not find a worthy companion,

> one should wander alone [*eka-* √*CAR*],
> like a king who has renounced the conquered realm,
> or like an elephant in the elephant-forest.[155]

The same goes for the *Khaggavisāṇasutta*: the renouncer should roam alone, fearless like the lion 'the king of beasts' (*rājā migānaṃ*), elephant, or rhinoceros:[156]

> Like an elephant, with a massive back, spotted, noble,
> who has left the herd, in order to dwell according to his will in the forest,
> one should wander alone [*eka-* √*CAR*] like the rhinoceros.[157]

Friends, family, and women must be forsaken,[158] for it is impossible to attain emancipation while enjoying company.[159] Yet, Richard Salomon argues, the "overall message of the *sutta* is not that one must have no companions at all, but rather that one should choose one's companions very carefully for their moral and spiritual merits."[160] Toward the end of the *sutta*, friendship (*metta*) is actually praised, but it is the friendliness toward *all* beings, the virtues of equanimity and non-violence, which comes

---

[154] *Mahābhārata* 12.105.51. The senior male elephant typically lives apart from the herd of female and young elephants.

[155] ... *rājā va raṭṭhaṃ vijitaṃ pahāya* | *eko care mātaṅgaraññe va nāgo* || (*Dhammapada* 329); similarly 61, 305, 330, 395; *Udāna* 4.5; *Suttanipāta* 46, 53. *Gāthā* 239 in Pali *Jātaka* 525 deals with a king who has renounced (*pabbajito*) and goes away like a solitary elephant (*nāgo va ekako carati*). Cf. Āryaśūra's *Jātakamālā* 30.1–4 about an elephant who is roaming alone in the forest, (peaceful) like an ascetic (*nāgavane ... ekacaro hastī ... tapasvīva*).

[156] *Khaggavisāṇasutta* 71–72.

[157] *nāgo va yūthāni vivajjayitvā* | *sañjātakhandho padumī ulāro* | *yathābhirantaṃ vihare araññe* | *eko care khaggavisāṇakappo* || (*Khaggavisāṇasutta* 53) 'Spotted' (*padumin-*) probably refers to the partial loss of pigmentation on senior elephants. Cf. Shulman 2012:390.

[158] *Khaggavisāṇasutta* 35–38, 41, 43, 49, 60.

[159] *saṃgaṇikāra-*, *Khaggavisāṇasutta* 54.

[160] Salomon 2000:7; *Khaggavisāṇasutta* 45; cf. 47, 57.

from *detachment*, not the friendship that means attachment to another person. If it is not possible to find an exceptionally noble companion one should roam about in solitude, like a king who has renounced his kingdom,[161] which reflects a recurrent motif in ancient Indian literature: the king who gives up his throne in order to seek *mokṣa*. Royal imagery may also hide behind verse 42: 'he who is in the four directions' (*cātuddisa*) refers to one who advances in all directions of space – the renouncer who is free to roam as he pleases, like the rhinoceros – but it could also reflect the Vedic ideal of the king as a conqueror of the four directions of space (*digvijaya*):

> (At home in) all directions [of space], unhindered anywhere,
> being satisfied with one thing or another,
> a bearer of dangers, fearless,
> one should wander alone [*eka-* √*CAR*] like the rhinoceros.[162]

Gāthā 48 of the *Khaggavisāṇasutta* uses the delicate simile of two bracelets, clashing against each other:[163] when a girl wears more than one bracelet they clash and make noise as she moves her arm, whereas the single bracelet remains quiet. This signifies that company should be avoided, as it leads to unnecessary talk and disturbances. The *gāthā* belongs to a set of verses known from the Pali *Jātaka* 408, which deals with four royal, pre-Śākyamuni *paccekabuddha*s, who realise the impermanence of everything in the world and renounce it.[164] According to Dhivan Jones, the existence of the *Khaggavisāṇasutta* in Pali, Gandhari, and Buddhist Hybrid-Sanskrit indicates its popularity among *bhikkhu*s, but "the attribution from early times of the rhinoceros stanzas to the

---

[161] *Khaggavisāṇasutta* 46, as in *Dhammapada* 329 above.

[162] *cātuddiso appaṭigho ca hoti | santussamāno itarītarena | parissayānaṃ sahitā achambhī | eko care khaggavisāṇakappo ||* (*Khaggavisāṇasutta* 42, translation by Salomon 2000:174–175)

[163] *disvā suvaṇṇassa pabhassarāni | kammāraputtena suniṭṭhitāni | saṃghaṭṭamānāni duve bhujasmiṃ | eko care khaggavisāṇakappo ||* "Having seen the two golden (bracelets), brilliant, well-made by the smith's son, clashing against each other on the arm, one should wander alone like the rhinoceros." (*Khaggavisāṇasutta* 48)

[164] Norman 1983:82; Salomon 2000:8–9; cf. *Mahāvastu* 1.301. On the debated term and concept of *paccekabuddha* see, for example, Anālayo 2010.

paccekabuddhas [who lived long ago], evident in the *Mahāvastu* as well as in the *Apadāna* and *Cūlaniddesa* [Pali commentary], suggests that the solitary lifestyle recommended by the stanzas seemed to the early Buddhists not to be an ideal to which they could practically aspire."[165]

Finally, one can mention the *Munisutta* (*Suttanipāta* 207–221), which characterises the *muni* as a solitary wanderer and emphasises the necessity of leaving domestic life, echoing the sentiment of the Vedic Song of the Wanderer.[166] There are similar passages in the *Moneyyasutta* (*Suttanipāta* 699–723), the *Arindamajātaka* of the *Mahāvastu*,[167] Āryaśūra's *Jātakamālā*,[168] and the *Theragāthās*. The latter include, for example, a stanza attributed to Sītavaniya praising the solitary forest mendicant,[169] as well as verses attributed to Tissakumāra Ekavihāriya 'lone-dweller'. The latter describe the eremitical, sylvan life as nothing but pleasant and peaceful[170] – bear in mind the lyrical element in some *Theragāthās* – not harsh and physically painful as in the more realistic *Uttarajjhayaṇa* (15.4) and *Khaggavisāṇasutta* (52).

Many of the verses in the Pali texts mentioned here are not distinctly Buddhist. They present an archaic type of pre-monastic, pre-sectarian ascetic poetry, reminiscent of the Song of the Wanderer.

---

165 Jones 2014:176.

166 *Suttanipāta* 207–208, 213; cf. 821, *Udāna* 3.9; *Mahābhārata* 12.237.22 (*munim .... ekacaraṃ*), 12.316.23–24 (*ekacaryārataḥ ... eko ramate muniḥ*); Shulman 2012:392f.

167 When asked by king Arindama about the ascetic life, the *paccekabuddha* Sronaka replied: "O king, what is a kingdom to a man who fares all alone [*ekasya carato*]? This is the first blessing of the poor, homelss monk [*adhanasya anāgārasya bhikṣuṇo*]." (*Mahāvastu* 3.452, translation by Jones 1943) The story is based on the Pali *Sonakajātaka* (number 529).

168 *Jātakamālā* 21.11–12: "In cremation-grounds, deserted areas, mountains, or forests teeming with fierce wild animals, abandoning their houses, ascetics dwell wherever they are at sunset. Intent on meditation and constantly wandering alone [*ekacarāś*], they withdraw from the sight of women..." (translation based on Meiland 2009)

169 *Theragāthā* 6; cf. 95 and 245.

170 *Theragāthā* 537–540 and 543–544.

VI. How much of this reflects the historical reality?

Now, the reader may wonder how much of all this high talk of living in solitude and walking constantly reflects historical reality? This is not easy to determine. We know that there were no monasteries in India when the Buddhist and Jaina ascetic orders were formed, and the texts describe how Śākyamuni, Mahāvīra, and their disciples visited and taught in various parks and similar localities.[171] When we acknowledge the similarities between the Pali/Prakrit *gāthās*/*gāhās* and the Song of the Wanderer, it seems probable that by the mid 1st millennium BCE the ideal of the solitary wandering ascetic was already firmly established. From this time, especially towards the end of the 1st millennium BCE, various ascetic groups (Buddhist, Jaina, Brahmanic) shared this ideal.

Both Śākyamuni and Mahāvīra organized their disciples in orders – perhaps because, as Stanley Tambiah writes, the personal quest of the renouncer was thought to be best undertaken in a community of like-minded.[172] In a monastic environment it becomes necessary to find a space where one can be alone – if not physically then at least mentally and spiritually. *Viveka* 'seclusion' is highly esteemed in early Buddhist texts.[173] Śākyamuni differentiated between physical/outer and spiritual/inner solitude, the latter being more important, whereas the former could be realized temporarily.[174] "Canonical texts describe monks who had not reached the stage of Arahant, as well as great disciples and the Buddha himself, living alone at times, or with one, two or a few companions".[175]

The solitary wandering mendicant clearly contrasts with the *bhikkhu* who stays permanently at a monastery. The contrast is

---

171 Shiraishi 1996:150–158; Pieruccini 2018.

172 Tambiah 1981.

173 Anālayo 2009. Cf. *Dhammapada* 205, *Suttanipāta* 257.

174 Wijayaratna 1990:111–117. Physical seclusion forms the basis for mental seclusion (*citta-viveka*), but the highest is seclusion from defilements, which is reached in final liberation (Anālayo 2009; cf. Hudson 1976).

175 Wijayaratna 1990:111; cf. *Mahāvagga* 1.12 (Śākyamuni in solitary secluded meditation, *rahogata- paṭisallīna-*); Dutt 1924:110f.; Shiraishi 1996:158–159, 162, 166, 191–192 (*eka, ekavihārī, vijanavāta, vivitta*). Śākyamuni is said to have regularly gone into seclusion, for as long as up to 3 months (Anālayo 2009).

also stark between ascetic *gāthā*-poetry and Buddhist monastic literature, which presents the monk as "caught in a web of social and ritual obligations".[176] The domestication of monks is partly related to the influence of Buddhist lay people, who seek the merit that comes from supporting monks; for it is in the laity's interest that monks are easily accessible in permanently settled communities.[177] Daniel Boucher describes domestication and ascetic reform as a recurring pattern in monastic culture; the solitary or "eremitical" ideal never loses its attractiveness for new generations of ascetics:

> Buddhist reclusion has long struggled between two poles: the untamed renunciant on the outermost fringes of human civilization, an ascetic who earned his reputation from years of austerity; and the domesticated monk, sedentary and respectable, perhaps scholarly, but more often a ritual specialist attuned to the needs of the laity. These two poles, of course, are essentially coterminous with Weber's charismatic and bureaucratic modes of leadership. ... [I]t was the very success of wilderness-dwelling monks in acquiring patronage that eventually compromised this ascetic thrust. This dialectic – reform, domestication, and renewed reform – is a recurring pattern in monastic culture everywhere.[178]

It seems highly likely that the mendicant ideal, expressed in the *gāthā*s I have presented, reflects the real-life conditions of many ascetics around the mid 1st millennium BCE: they were wandering about alone or in small groups, from place to place, except during the rainy season. The earliest Buddhist order has been described as "a dispersed body of wandering hermits".[179] We should bear in mind that the ascetic poetry, although expressing high ideals,[180] discards poetic refinery and imagination; the *gāthā*s

[176] Lopez 2007:33.

[177] Bailey & Mabbett 2003:10.

[178] Boucher 2011:218–219. See Carrithers 1983 (on Singhalese monks); Prebish 1995 (on the sylvan renunciate ideal); Bailey & Mabbett 2003:87, 178–179 (on Thai monks).

[179] Dutt 1924:183; similarly Nakamura 1987:59; Bronkhorst 1993:99–100; Shiraishi 1996:160; Bailey & Mabbett 2003:165–168.

[180] Shulman sees the *Khaggavisāṇasutta* not as "an historical statement, but an idealized picture" of what "the author(s) felt the life of a recluse could be like." (2012:391)

are not intended to be mere words, but to function as guidance and self-instruction for one seeking the highest goal. Moreover, realistic botanical and faunal references in the verses, as well as references to vagabond-professions, suggest direct experience of life on road and trail. It is not difficult to imagine the easily memorized verses of the Song of the Wanderer, or the *Khaggavisāṇasutta*, being recited by ascetics while on the move.

As time went by, the ideal of solitary wandering became increasingly distanced from the real-life of Buddhist monks, as monasteries were built, and was viewed with nostalgia or projected onto a pre-Śākyamuni age of *paccekabuddha*s. Yet, from time to time, there appeared reformers who reacted against the domestication of the ascetic order and sought a more eremitical or mobile way of life. To some extent, the Brahmanic and Jaina renouncer-traditions were more successful than the Buddhist one in keeping alive itinerancy.[181] Even today, Indian *sādhus* spend much of their life on the road; they tend to spend their first period as *sādhus* travelling, then settle down at some pilgrimage-site and form congregations, rather than live as solitary wanderers.[182] Within Jainism, a more settled lifestyle developed around temple-complexes, while sylvan mendicants (*vanavāsī*s) continued to be wanderers. Today, although Mahāvīra's solitary lifestyle is seen as ideal, *bhikkhu*s usually live in groups (*gaṇa*s). Except during the rainy season, when they stay at shelters, Jaina mendicants walk tirelessly from one locality to another.[183]

VII. Final words

One can conclude that there are profound similarities between late Vedic, neo-Brahmanic, early Jaina, and early Buddhist *gāthā*-poetry on the benefits of wandering alone (*eka* + √*CAR*). Not only would Indra's "Song of the Wanderer" fit fairly well among the *gāthā*s of the *Suttanipāta* or the *Uttarajjhayaṇa*, but

181 Olivelle states that in the medieval period the ideal of ceaseless wandering was maintained, even when most ascetics resided in monasteries (1995:18; 2007:177–178).

182 Hausner 2007:95–107.

183 Caillat 1989:101.

the *role* of Indra, too, brings to mind the Buddhist and Jaina Indra (Śakra, Sakka, sometimes in the disguise of a *brāhmaṇa*), as tester, friend, even worshipper, of ascetics. Since Rohita is a *kṣatriya* on the threshold of adulthood, it is only fitting that the prototypical *kṣatriya* Indra establishes a relationship with him, but in addition to that we should recognize the common traits of warrior and ascetic – for, as we have seen, already in the early Vedic period Indra is associated with the lone hero and the ascetic. The common traits here are heroic conquest (exertion on the battlefield and in self-overcoming) and solar attributes.

The Sun functions as prototype of both the solitary wanderer/ascetic and the hero/ruler. The spatial movement of the Sun signifies conquest and tireless exertion.[184] The attributes of king and hero are projected on the renouncer as having unlimited spatial freedom and as spiritual conqueror (*jina, vīra*). The concept of *digvijaya* or 'conquest of the quarters of space' derives from the Vedic royal ritual, in which a tour in the corners of the land is undertaken by the victorious *kṣatriya*. In traditional hagiographies of Ādi-Śaṅkarācārya, this term is applied to his metaphysical conquest of India's four corners, as renouncer and scholar, which demonstrates the "complementarity of royal and ascetic paradigms in traditional India."[185]

The physical solitude of the ideal renouncer, and his detachment from society – though dependent on it for his bodily sustenance – mirrors his ultimate goal: *nirvāṇa*, *mokṣa*, also known as *kaivalya*, which translates as 'absolute isolation'.[186] This goal can only be attained individually, not collectively.[187] Paradoxical though it may seem, the homeless, wandering renouncer, engaged in nearly constant movement in the spatial world, is precisely the person who is supposed to have attained a state of

---

[184] Olivelle 2007:186. There is a *śloka* attributed to Bhartṛhari which compares a solitary hero, who conquers all land touched by his feet, with the Sun, whose rays reach the entire Earth (*Nītiśataka* 108 in Kāle & Gurjar; Miscellaneous 15 in Gopalachariar).

[185] Bader 2000:xii, 139, 169; cf. Burghart 1983:376–378. On similar Jaina views see Dundas 1991. The celibate is attributed freedom of movement in all worlds in *Chāndogyopaniṣad* 8.4.3, 8.5.4.

[186] Compare Latin *absolūtus* 'absolute, complete, freed, independent'.

[187] *Sūyagaḍa* (1.)2.3.16–17, (1.)10.12, (1.)13.18; Schneider 1960.

true rest. His course is "trackless".[188] The opposite of the sagely renouncer is the ignorant man who feels at home in this world; he too 'wanders about' (√*BHRAM*), but in circles[189] – "bound, revolving like a wheel (in movement)"[190], in "the circular path of birth and death"[191] – unable, the texts assert, to make the trans-saṃsāric leap.

References

Texts

Aitareyabrāhmaṇa: Aufrecht, Theodor. 1879. *Das Aitareyabrāhmaṇa*. Bonn.

Haug, Martin. 1863. *Aitareya Brāhmaṇam of the Rigveda... Edited, Translated and Explained... I. Sanscrit Text...* Bombay: Government Central Book Depôt / London: Trübner & Co.

Āyāra: Yuvācārya Mahāprajna & Muni Mahendra Kumār. 1981. *Āyāro (Ācārāṅga Sūtra), the First Aṅga Āgama (Canonical Text) of the Jainas: Text, Transl., Commentary* [based on the text of Muni Śrī Nathmaljī]. Jain Canonical Text Series 1. New Delhi: Today and Tomorrow's Printers and Publishers.

---

[188] The ascetic's course (*gati-*, *pada-*) is trackless, invisible (*na dṛśyeta*), like that of birds in the air and fish in the sea (*Mahābhārata* 12.154.28, 12.174.19, 12.231.24). Olivelle notes that the term *gati* can refer to the final goal, liberation, but also to "the way an ascetic is expected to go about in the world. He leaves no trail. He travels unnoticed and without a destination." (2012:98)

[189] *bhogī bhamai saṃsāre* | *abhogī vippamuccai* || "The voluptuary/enjoyer wanders about in *saṃsāra*; the non-enjoyer is liberated." (*Uttarajjhayaṇa* 25.41).

[190] *baddho bhramati cakravat* (*Mahābhārata* 12.287.19; similarly 12.316.57: *paribhramati saṃsāraṃ cakravad*), referring to one who is ignorant of *mokṣadharma*. *Vairāgyaśataka* of Bhartṛhari, verse 70 (Gopalachariar): You roam (*bhramasi*), from the lowest region to the highest, but is still ignorant of *bráhman* which leads to *nirvṛtti* ('cessation, rest, abstaining from worldly acts'). In verse 39 the ordinary man is said to wander around (*paribhramati*) in *saṃsāra*. The use of √*BHRAM* in these verses can mean 'to wander about', but also 'to circulate', and 'to move unsteadily, err, confuse' (cf. Āryaśūra's *Jātakamālā* 6.34–38).

[191] *jāi-maraṇassa vaḍumagaṃ* (*Āyāra* 5.[6.]122), which the *muṇi* transcends.

Bhartṛhari: Kāle, M. R. & Gurjar, M. B. 1898. *The Nītiśataka and Vairāgyaśataka of Bhartṛhari: Edited with Notes and an English Translation.* Bombay: Gopāl Nārāyan & Co.

Gopalachariar, A. V. 1954. *Bhartrihari's Sringara Sataka and Vairagya Sataka with Sanskrit Commentary, English Notes, Translation and Introduction.* Madras: V. Ramaswamy Sastrulu & Sons.

Corpus Inscriptionum Indicarum: Hultzsch, E. 1925. *Corpus Inscriptionum Indicarum. I: Inscriptions of Asoka.* Oxford: Clarendon Press.

Dhammapada: Norman, K.R. & von Hinüber, O. 1994. *Dhammapada: Edited.* Oxford: Pali Text Society

Dīghanikāya: Rhys-Davids, D. & Carpenter, E. 1890. *Dīghanikāya: Edited.* London: Pali Text Society.

Jātaka: Fausbøll, V. 1877 [1962]. *The Jātaka together with its Commentary... Edited in the Original Pāli.* London: Pali Text Society.

Jātakamālā of Āryaśūra: Meiland, Justin. 2009. *Garland of the Buddha's Past Lives, by Aryashura. Vol. II: Translated [with Text].* Clay Sanskrit Library. New York: New York University Press.

Jaiminīyabrāhmaṇa: Bodewitz, H. W. 1973. *Jaiminīya Brāhmaṇa 1, 1–65: Translation and Commentary with a Study 'Agnihotra and Prāṇāgnihotra'.* Leiden: Brill.

Jiṇacaritta (= Book 1 of "Kalpasūtra"): Jacobi, Hermann. 1879. *The Kalpasûtra of Bhadrabâhu: Edited with an Introduction, Notes and... Glossary.* Abhandlungen für die Kunde des Morgenlandes 7 (1). Leipzig: F. A. Brockhaus.

——— 1884 [1980]. *Jaina Sûtras I: Translated...* Sacred Books of the East 22. Delhi: Motilal Banarsidass.

Stevenson, J. 1848. *The Kalpa Sútra and Nava Tatva, two Works Illustrative of the Jain Religion and Philosophy: Translated from the Mágadhí. With an Appendix containing Remarks on the Language of the Original.* London: Oriental Translation Fund of Great Britain.

Mahābhārata, Bombay edition: [Board of scholars.] VS 2013–2015. *Śrīman Mahābhāratam. I–IV.* Gorakhpur: Gita Press.

Mahābhārata, Critical edition: Sukthankar, Vishnu S. *et alii*. 1933–1966. *The Mahābhārata: For the First Time Critically Edited. I–XIX*. Poona: Bhandarkar Oriental Research Institute.

Mahāvagga: Oldenberg, Hermann. 1879. *The Vinaya Piṭakaṃ... Edited. I: The Mahāvagga*. London: Williams and Norgate.

Mahāvastu: Jones, J. 1943. *Mahāvastu: Edited*. London: Pali Text Society.

Manusmṛti: Olivelle, Patrick. 2005. *Manu's Code of Law: A Critical Edition and Translation...* Oxford: Oxford University Press.

Ovavāiya: Leumann, Ernst. 1883. *Das Aupapâtika Sûtra, erstes Upânga der Jaina. 1: Einleitung, Text und Glossar*. Abhandlungen für die Kunde des Morgenlandes, DMG 7 (2). Leipzig.

Lalwani, Ganesh & Ramesh Muni Shastri & K. C. Lalwani. 1988. *Uvavāiya Suttam (Aupapātika Sūtraṃ)*. [Text with Hindi and English Transl.] Prakrit Bharati Publication 50. Jaipur: Prakrit Bharati Academy.

Pañcamāśramavidhi: See Olivelle 2012 below.

Ṛgvedasaṃhitā: Aufrecht, Theodor. 1877. *Die Hymnen des Ṛigveda. I–II*. Zweite Auflage. Bonn: Adolph Marcus.

Śāṅkhāyanaśrautasūtra: Tokunaga, Muneo. 1995. "Śāṅkhāyana Śrautasūtra". GRETIL. Electronic text, based on the edition by A. Hillebrandt, Calcutta 1885–1899, Bibliotheca Indica 99.

Śatapathabrāhmaṇa-Mādhyandina: Weber, Albecht. 1855. *The Çatapatha-Brâhmaṇa in the Mâdhyandina-Çâkhâ...: Edited*. Berlin: Ferd. Dümmler's Verlagsbuchhandlung / London: Williams & Norgate.

Śaunakīyasaṃhitā: Roth, R. & Whitney, W. D. 1924 [1966]. *Atharva Veda Sanhita*. Dritte unveränderte Auflage... Bonn: Ferd. Dümmlers Verlag.

Griffith, Ralph. 1895–1896. *Hymns of the Atharva-Veda: Translated. I–II*. Benares: Lazarus & Co.

Sūyagaḍa: Yamasaki, M. & Ousaka, Y. 1997. Sūyagaḍa: Version 1.2. Romanised text of the critical ed. by P. L. Vaidya (*Sūyagaḍam*, Poona 1928), metre analysis, and indexes.

Jacobi, Hermann. 1895 [1980]. *Jaina Sûtras II: Translated...* Sacred Books of the East 45. Delhi: Motilal Banarsidass.

Suttanipāta: Andersen, D. & Smith, H. 1913. *Sutta-Nipāta: Edited.* London: Pali Text Society.

Taittirīyabrāhmaṇa: Dumont, Paul-Emil. 1948. The Horse-Sacrifice in the Taittirīya-Brāhmaṇa: The Eighth and Ninth Prapāṭhakas of the Third Kāṇḍa of the Taittirīya-Brāhmaṇa with Translation. *Proceedings of the American Philosophical Society* 92 (6), 447–503.

Theragāthā: Oldenberg, Hermann & Pischel, Richard. 1883 [1966]. *The Thera- and Therî-Gâthâ...: Edited.* 2nd ed. with appendices by K. R. Norman & L. Alsdorf 1966. London: Pali Text Society.

Udāna: Steinthal, Paul. 1885 [1948]. *Udāna: Edited.* London: Pali Text Society.

Uttarajjhayaṇa: Charpentier, Jarl. 1921–1922. *The Uttarādhyayanasūtra: Edited. I–II.* Archives D'Études Orientales 18:1–2. Leipzig: Harassowitz.

Vājasaneyisaṃhitā: [*sine nomine*]. 1957. *Vājasaneyi-saṃhitā.* Pārḍī.

Yatidharmasamuccaya: Olivelle, Patrick. 1995. *Rules and Regulations of Brahmanical Asceticism. Yatidharmasamuccaya of Yādava Prakāśa: Edited and Translated.* New York: State University of New York Press.

Literature

Alsdorf, Ludwig. 1963. "Uttarajjhāyā Studies". In: *Indo-Iranian Journal* 6, 110–136.

Anālayo, Bhikkhu. 2009. "*Viveka*". In: Weeraratne, W. G. (ed.), *Encyclopaedia of Buddhism*, 720–722.

——— 2010. "Paccekabuddhas in the Isigili-sutta and its Ekottarika-āgama Parallel". In: *Canadian Journal of Buddhist Studies* 6, 5–36.

Ānandajoti, Bhikkhu. 2013. "An Outline of the Metres in the Pāḷi Canon". Version 3.6. (An earlier version was published in *Indologica Taurinensia* 36, 2000.)

Bader, Jonathan. 2000. *Conquest of the Four Quarters: Traditional Accounts of the Life of Śaṅkara.* New Delhi: Aditya Prakashan.

Bailey, Greg & Mabbett, Ian. 2003. *The Sociology of Early Buddhism*. Cambridge: Cambridge University Press.

Boucher, Daniel. 2011. "Sacrifice and Asceticism in Early Mahāyāna Buddhism". In: Lindquist, S. (ed.), *Religion and Identity in South Asia and Beyond*, London: Anthem Press, 197–223.

Bronkhorst, Johannes. 1993 [2000]. *The Two Traditions of Meditation in Ancient India*. 2nd ed. Delhi: Motilal Banarsidass.

Burghart, Richard. 1983. "Wandering Ascetics of the Rāmānandī Sect". In: *History of Religions* 22 (4), 361–380.

Caillat, Colette. 1989. "Jainism". In: Kitagawa, J. (ed.), *The Religious Traditions of Asia*, London: Routledge, 97–109.

———2003. "Gleanings from a Comparative Reading of Early Canonical Buddhist and Jaina Texts". In: *Journal of the International Association of Buddhist Studies* 26 (2), 25–50.

Carrithers, Michael. 1983. *The Forest Monks of Sri Lanka: An Anthropological and Historical Study*. Delhi: Oxford University Press.

Charpentier, Jarl. 1910. "Zu Uttarajjhayaṇa XXV". In: *Wiener Zeitschrift für die Kunde des Morgenlandes* 24, 62–69.

Dore, Moreno. 2015. "The Ekavrātya, Indra and the Sun". In: Pontillo, T. *et alii* (eds.), *The Volatile World of Sovereignty: The Vrātya Problem and Kingship in South Asia*, New Delhi: D.K. Printworld, 33–64.

Dundas, Paul. 1991. "The Digambara Jain Warrior". In: Carrithers, M. & Humphrey, C. (eds.), *The Assembly of Listeners: Jains in Society*. Cambridge: Cambridge University Press, 169–186.

Dutt, Sukumar. 1924. *Early Buddhist Monachism, 600–100 BC*. London: Keagan Paul.

Falk, Harry. 1984. "Die Legede von Śunaḥśepa vor ihrem rituellen Hintergrund". In: *Zeitschrift der Deutschen Morgenländischen Gesellschaft* 134 (1), 115–135.

Hausner, Sondra. 2007. *Wandering with Sadhus: Ascetics in the Hindu Himalayas*. Bloomington & Indianapolis: Indiana University Press.

Horsch, Paul. 1966. *Die vedische Gāthā- und Śloka-Literatur*. Bern: Francke Verlag.

Hudson, Malcolm. 1976. "Note on Solitude/Inwardness". In: *Pali Buddhist Review* 1 (1), 103–104.

Ireland, John D. 1997. *Vaṅgīsa: An Early Buddhist Poet.* Buddhist Publication Society. The Wheel Publication 417. [Access to Insight edition 2005.]

Jayawickrama, N.A. 1977. "A Critical Analysis of the Suttanipāta: Uraga, Khaggavisāṇa and Muni Suttas". In: *Pali Buddhist Review* 2.1, 14–41.

Jones, Dhivan Thomas. 2014. "Like the Rhinoceros, or Like Its Horn? The Problem of Khaggavisāṇa Revisited". In: *Buddhist Studies Review* 31 (2), 165–178.

Lienhard, Siegfried. 1984a. *A History of Classsical Poetry: Sanskrit – Pali – Prakrit.* A History of Indian Literature 3:1. Wiesbaden: Otto Harrassowitz.

Lopez, Donald S., Jr. 2007 [1995]. "Introduction". In: Lopez, D. (ed.), *Buddhism in Practice.* Abridged edition. Princeton: Princeton University Press, 3–34.

McGovern, Nathan. 2019. *The Snake and the Mongoose: The Emergence of Identity in Early Indian Religion.* Oxford: Oxford University Press.

Nāgapriya, Dharmacāri. 2004. "Pre-Doctrinal Buddhism in the Sutta-Nipāta: A Psychological Portrait of the Early Buddhist Saint". *Western Buddhist Review* 4: http://www.westernbuddhistreview.com/vol4/Early%20Buddhist%20Saint2.pdf

Nakamura, Hajime. 1983. "Common Elements in Early Jain and Buddhist Literature". In: *Indologica Taurinensia 9 (Proceedings of the International Symposium on Jaina Canonical and Narrative Literature, Strasbourg 1981)*, 303–330.

——— 1987. *Indian Buddhism.* Delhi: Motilal Banarsidass.

Norman, K.R. 1983. *Pāli Literature.* Wiesbaden: Otto Harrassowitz.

——— 1996. "Solitary as a Rhinoceros Horn". In: *Buddhist Studies Review* 13 (2), 133–142.

Oberlies, Thomas. 1997. "Veda-Schüler, Bettelasketen und Mönche: Zur 'Vorgeschichte' der buddhistischen Ordensregeln". Vortragsmanuskript, Universität Hamburg.

Olivelle, Patrick. 1974. *The Origin and the Early Development of Buddhist Monachism*. Colombo: Gunasena.

——— 2007. "On the Road: The Religious Significance of Walking". In: Byrski, M.K. & Nowakowska, M. *et alii* (eds.). *Theatrum Mirabiliorum Indiae Orientalis: A Volume to Celebrate the 70th Birthday of Professor Maria K. Byrski*. Warzawa: Dom Wydawniczy Elipsa, 173–187.

——— 2012. *Ascetics and Brahmins: Studies in Ideologies and Institutions*. London: Anthem Press.

Pieruccini, Cinzia. 2018. Travelling Śākyamuni, Groves, Reserves and Orchards". In: Stasik, Danuta & Trynkowska, Anna (eds.). 2018. *Journeys and Travellers in Indian Literature and Art. I–II*. Warzaw: Elipsa, 62–77.

Prebish, Charles. 1995. "Ideal Types in Indian Buddhism: A New Paradigm". In: *Journal of the American Oriental Society* 115 (4), 651–666.

Rau, Wilhelm. 1963. "Bemerkungen und nicht-Buddhistische Sanskrit-Parallelen zum Pāli-Dhammapada". In: Vogel (ed.), *Jñānamuktāvalī: Commemoration Volume in Honour of Johannes Nobel*, International Academy of Indian Culture, 159–175.

Revire, Nicolas. 2017. "Solar Symbolism in Early Buddhist Literature". In: *Berliner Indologische Studien* 23, 143–156.

Salomon, Richard. 2000. *A Gāndhārī Version of the Rhinoceros Sūtra: British Library Kharoṣṭhī Fragment 5B*. With a contribution by Andrew Glass. Seattle & London: University of Washington Press.

Schneider, Ulrich. 1960. "Der individualistische Zug im indischen Denken". In: Waldschmidt, Ernst (ed.), *Indologen-Tagung 1959: Verhandlungen der Indologischen Arbeitstagung in Essen-Bredeney, Villa Hügel 13.-15. Juli 1959*, Göttingen: Vandenhoeck & Ruprecht, 244–251.

Shiraishi, Ryokai. 1996. *Asceticism in Buddhism and Brahmanism: A Comparative Study*. Tring (UK): Institute of Buddhist Studies.

Shulman, Eviatar. 2012. "Early Buddhist Imagination: The Aṭṭhakavagga as Buddhist Poetry". In: *Journal of the International Association of Buddhist Studies* 35 (1–2), 363–411.

Tambiah, Stanley J. 1981. “The Renouncer’s Individuality and Community”. In: *Contributions to Indian Sociology* 15, 299–320.

Tatia, Nathmal & Kumar, Muni Mahendra. 1981. *Aspects of Jaina Monasticism*. Today and Tomorrow’s Printers and Publishers.

Upali Sramon. 2011. “Elements of a Buddhist Literary Theory as Depicted in Pali Literature”. In: *Journal of the Royal Asiatic Society of Sri Lanka, New Series* 57, 19–39.

Weller, Friedrich. 1956. “Die Legende von Śunaḥśepa im Aitareya-brāhmaṇa und Śāṅkhāyana-śrautasūtra”. In: *Berichte über die Verhandlungen der sächsischen Akademie der Wissenschaften zu Leipzig*. Band 102, Philol.-Hist. Klasse, Heft 2. Berlin.

Wijayaratna, Mohan. 1990. *Buddhist Monastic Life*. Cambridge: Cambridge University Press.

Wright, J.C. 2001. “The Gandhari Prakrit Version of the Rhinoceros Sūtra”. In: *Anusamdhan* 18, 1–15.

Zysk, Kenneth. 1998. *Asceticism and Healing in Ancient India: Medicine in the Buddhist Monastery*. Delhi: Motilal Banarsidass.

4. Milarepa Sings Again: Tsangnyön Heruka's 'Songs with Parting Instructions'

Stefan Larsson[192]

Abstract

Although Tibetan Buddhism is often associated with monks and canonical texts, other types of Buddhist practitioners and other kinds of texts are also of importance. Before the 5th Dalai Lama came to power in 1642 and Tibetan Buddhism became increasingly systematized and monastically oriented, Tibetan charismatic *yogin*s composed and printed religious poetry (*mgur*) and hagiographies (*rnam thar*) to promote a non-monastic ideal with remarkable success. They modelled their lifestyle upon Indian Tantric *siddha*s and on the Tibetan poet-saint Milarepa (c. 1040–1123). Like them, they adopted a wandering lifestyle and used religious poetry as a means for spreading their message. By expressing themselves through poetry, which they also composed, these yogins could present Buddhism in an innovative way, adapted to the needs of their audience. Taking the 'songs with parting instructions' (*'gro chos kyi mgur*) of the 'crazy yogin' (*rnal 'byor smyon pa*) Tsangnyön Heruka (1452–1507) as the point of departure, this chapter explores how these colourful figures attempted to

192 This chapter is based on a paper that I presented at the Fifteenth Seminar of the International Association for Tibetan Studies (IATS) in Paris, 2019. The main research upon which the chapter is based was carried out during a research project financed by the Swedish Research Council (project 2013–1421). I would like to express my gratitude to Margot and Rune Johansson's Foundation for a grant that enabled me to visit the IATS Seminar.

How to cite this book chapter:
Larsson, S. 2021. Milarepa Sings Again: Tsangnyön Heruka's 'Songs with Parting Instructions'. In: Larsson, S. and af Edholm, K. (eds.) *Songs on the Road: Wandering Religious Poets in India, Tibet, and Japan*. Pp. 67–92. Stockholm: Stockholm University Press. DOI: https://doi.org/10.16993/bbi.d.

vitalize Buddhism in Tibet by creating an alternative religious infrastructure outside of the monastery.

I. The songs of a wandering *yogin*

mGur (pronounced *gur*) denotes a specific type of religious poetry that has played an important role in the expression and transmission of Buddhism across the Tibetan cultural world.[193] The term *mgur* is usually translated as 'song' and it has been used to refer to a wide variety of oral and literary creations. However, the most common use of the term came to be that which referred to a more Buddhist type of song, associated with wandering *yogin*s and distinguished by a simple style, an emphasis on the experiential and the spontaneous, and a performative function. In this sense, *mgur* has commonly been contrasted with *snyan ngag* (Sanskrit *kāvya*), which denotes an ornamented, written, Indian-inspired form of poetry. There are several Tibetan terms that have been used as synonyms for *mgur*, such as *glu* and *dbyangs*. Milarepa (Mi la ras pa) was probably the most famous Tibetan composer of *mgur*.[194] There are, nevertheless, many other famous and popular *mgur*-composers and the tradition of composing and performing *mgur* remains popular throughout the Tibetan cultural region. The roots of these songs go back both to Indian *siddha*-songs and to Tibetan folk-songs.[195]

---

[193] This paragraph is a slightly revised version of an abstract for a panel about songs of realization in Tibetan culture that I organized together with Carl Yamamoto at the IATS Seminar in Paris 2019. The paragraph was co-written with Yamamoto. For studies of songs in the Tibetan tradition, see Ardussi 1977; Jackson 1996; Larsson & Quintman 2015; Sørensen 1990; Sujata 2005; Yamamoto 2015. For English translations of such songs, see for example Jinpa & Elsner 2000; Nālandā Translation Committee 1986 and1989; Stearns 2000 and 2012; Sujata 2005 and 2012.

[194] When Tibetan names occur in the running text of the article they are given as they are pronounced, with their spelling provided in parenthesis the first time the name occurs. When Tibetan terms and names occur in parentheses they are provided according to spelling. Specific terms, such as *mgur*, are spelled out also in the running text.

[195] For studies of *siddha*-songs, see for example Braitstein 2014; Guenther 1969; Jackson 2004; Kapstein 2006; Kværne 1977; Schaeffer 2005; Templeman 1994. For an overview of religious poetry and Buddhist songs in

In 1488 the crazy yogin Tsangnyön Heruka compiled and printed two texts that became enormously popular and influential in Tibetan cultural areas and beyond: a hagiography of Milarepa (*Mi la'i rnam thar*) and a collection of songs attributed to Milarepa (*Mi la'i mgur 'bum*).[196] These two texts are regarded as classics of world literature. The texts have been reprinted again and again, and translated into numerous languages. In these texts Milarepa's constant wanderings are described in a dramatic, captivating, beautiful, and oftentimes humorous way. The two texts complement each other and are sometimes printed together. Both texts contain many religious songs (*mgur*) that are attributed to Milarepa. It is said in the hagiography that Milarepa had an exceptionally beautiful voice, which he made use of when explaining what he believed to be important and helpful to people he encountered. Milarepa never became a monk but preferred to live outside of the confines of monasteries, wandering between isolated caves in the wilderness where he practiced meditation under austere and harsh circumstances. Both in the hagiography and in the song-collection, learned monks are often portrayed in a negative way, as jealous and greedy antagonists of Milarepa. The life of Milarepa ends when a covetous monk poisons him to death. Tsangnyön based his version of the life and songs upon a large body of stories and religious poems about the cotton-clad yogin, stories that had been existing for centuries. He did,

---

the Tibetan tradition, see Jackson 1996; Larsson & Quintman 2015:87–97; Stein 1988 [1972]:248–276. For a study about *mgur* written by a Tibetan scholar, see Don grub rgyal 1997.

[196] For more information about Tsangnyön Heruka, see for example Larsson 2012 and 2019b; for more information about crazy yogins in Tibet, see for example Larsson 2019a. The collected songs (*mgur 'bum*) of Milarepa which Tsangnyön compiled and printed is available in English translation in Chang 1989 and in Tsangnyön 2017. Tsangnyön's disciple Lhatsun Rinchen Namgyel compiled and printed Milarepa songs that were not include in Tsangnyön's collection. These have been translated to English by Kunga & Cutillo (1986; 1995 [1978]). For a study of Tsangnyön's version of Milarepa's hagiography (*rnam thar*), which also situates the text within the wider biographical tradition of Milarepa, see Quintman 2014. For English translations of Tsangnyön's version of Milarepa's life story, see Evans-Wentz 2000 [1928]; Lhalungpa 1979 [1977]; Tsangnyön 2010. For a critical edition of the text, see Jong 1959.

however, present the material in an, at the time, novel fashion, thus making the story and songs more accessible and concordant than many of the older versions. He also made certain innovations, the *bonpo*-priest that poisons Milarepa to death in some of the older version becomes a learned monk, a so-called *geshe* (*dge bshes*), for example.[197]

Twenty years after Tsangnyön had compiled and printed the two works on Milarepa, in 1508, one year after his passing, some of Tsangnyön Heruka's disciples gathered in Southern Latö (La stod lho) where they collected and printed their beloved master's songs and biography along with two other texts that are related to Tsangnyön.[198] Tsangnyön's songs are a testimony of his mastery of composing *mgur*, and given his importance for Tibetan literature, it is somewhat surprising that his songs have remained relatively unknown, both among Tibetans and in Western Tibetological scholarship. Tsangnyön's songs provide us with insight to the way in which he taught Dharma to his disciples. They also offer fascinating glimpses of the wandering yogic lifestyle that he and many of his disciples followed and propagated. As might be expected, Tsangnyön's songs resembles those of Milarepa, both in style and contents.

It is noteworthy that Tsangnyön's song-collection is similar to a life-story in some ways, beginning with the first song that he sang in his late twenties in Lachi (La phyi), the collection covers his adult life and ends with his last words, words that he uttered before passing away in Rechungpuk (Ras chung phug) at age 55. The songs are ordered chronologically, and each song is surrounded by a narrative frame providing the context around the song. The song-collection is 28 folios long and contains 27 songs of varying length; six of the songs are called major songs

---

[197] *Bon* is a religion that existed in Tibet before Buddhism. *Bonpo* the name of a follower of the *Bon* religion.

[198] This printing endeavour has been described by Ehrhard 2010; Sernesi 2011a. The four texts are described in Larsson 2016. The title of the song-collection that they produced at that time is *The Collection of the Songs of the Master Heruka from Tsang: The Wish-fulfilling Jewel Showing the Path of the All-Knowing One* (*rJe btsun gtsang pa he ru ka'i mgur 'bum rin po che dbang gi rgyal po thams cad mkhyen pa'i lam ston*). The text is also available in some private collections. I recently published a Swedish translation of the text (Larsson 2018).

(*mgur chen*), a term that indicates that these songs were regarded as particularly important or perhaps that they were especially popular and well-known at the time.[199]

Tsangnyön's songs were later (in 1512 and 1543) incorporated in two hagiographies, authored by his disciples Götsangrepa (rGod tshang ras pa, 1482–1559) and Lhatsun Rinchen Namgyel (lHa btsun Rin chen rnam rgyal,1473–1557), respectively.[200] Ngödrub Pembar (dNgos grub dpal 'bar, 1456–1527), whose hagiography about Tsangnyön was printed along with the song-collection, do not include the songs.[201] Götsangrepa categorizes Tsangnyön's songs into four main types in a short catalogue of the song-collection that likely was printed alongside with the song-collection itself, and thus constitutes one of the above mentioned four texts that were printed in 1508:[202]

- Instructional songs (*gdams pa'i mgur*)
- Songs that introduces [the mind] (*ngo sprod kyi mgur*)
- Question-and-answer songs (*zhus lan gi mgur*)
- Songs with parting instructions (*'gro chos kyi mgur*)

---

199 The actual number of songs is larger: some songs that are counted as one actually contain several related songs, and two songs are attributed to other persons. The term *mgur chen* is also used for some of Marpa's songs in the hagiography that Tsangnyön printed in 1505. Nālandā Translation Committee translates the term as "grand song" (Nālandā 1986:43).

200 rGod tshang ras pa, *Nyi ma'i snying po*; lHa btsun Rin chen rnam rgyal, *Dad pa'i spu slong g.yo ba*. Götsangrepa includes all the songs in his version, and besides some peculiar spellings, he renders the songs almost as the song-collection does, and in a similar order. Lhatsun leaves out several songs and sometimes provides verses that are not found in the other texts. He also divides one song and makes two separate songs out of it, which seem logical when looking at the song in question. It is notable that Lhatsun was not involved in printing the song-collection, so it is not surprising that his version of the songs differs. However, the differences indicate that the songs could have been available in different versions and that Lhatsun might had access to other versions of the same songs. David DiValerio (2015) writes about the connection between these texts. When rendering variant spellings in the Tibetan sources in the notes, L indicate Lhatsun's and G indicate Götsangrepa's hagiographies of Tsangnyön.

201 dNgos grub dpal 'bar, *Dad pa'i seng ge*.

202 *The Illuminating Sunbeam Catalogue* (*dKar chags nyi 'od snang ba*). For a Swedish translation of this text, see Larsson 2018:201–203.

These different categories are not clearly distinguishable. For example, most of the songs are instructional songs, in some sense, and many of the songs are question-and-answer songs in so far that they are performed in response to questions from disciples. There are also some other types of songs included in the collection, for example a song about how to interpret a dream (*rmi lam brda 'grol kyi mgur*).

II. Tsangnyön's 'songs with parting instructions'

The present chapter will explore the 'songs with parting instructions' (*'gro chos kyi mgur*) that are found in the song-collection. A song with parting instructions is a song that Tsangnyön sings to a disciple who is about to leave for a longer journey. Such a song contains instructions and advise that the disciple needs to keep in mind while being away from his or her teacher.[203] This type of song is especially relevant for the present discussion, since it often describes the non-monastic and wandering lifestyle that Tsangnyön advocated and followed.

The first song with parting instructions appears on the front-side of folio 12 of the song-collection.[204] In the prose introduction that is given before the song begins, the context of the song is provided. According to this narrative frame surrounding the song, the song was written down in a letter, which Tsangnyön sent in response to a letter that he had received from the female ruler of Tenkheb (gTeng khebs),[205] Sönam Sangmo (bSod rnams bzang mo). Sönam Sangmo was one of many dignitaries who had a teacher–patron relationship (*yon mchod*) with Tsangnyön.[206] In

[203] The term is somewhat difficult to translate. Feedback from Tibetan scholars that I received at IATS seminar 2019 and discussions with Khenpo Chödrak Tenpel in August 2019 have, along with the contents of the songs and the contexts around them, helped me to get an idea of what the term means. Khenpo Chödrak also said that the term can be used when the *lama* is leaving for a journey and his disciples remain.

[204] This song is rendered in gTsang smyon, *gTsang pa he ru ka'i mgur 'bum*:12a–13a. Cf. rGod tshang ras pa, *Nyi ma'i snying po*:92–93; lHa btsun Rin chen rnam rgyal, *Dad pa'i spu slong g.yo ba*:87–89.

[205] Tenkheb probably refers to Tingkheb (*gTing khebs*), a place situated 83 km from Sakya (thanks to Hildegard Diemberger for this suggestion).

[206] See Ruegg 1997, for more information about teacher–patron relationships.

her letter Sönam Sangmo had written that she was in a difficult situation since her planned wedding with the ruler of Tsamda (Tshwa mda') had been cancelled, due to the Tsamda ruler's sudden death. Now she did not know what to do and was on her way back to her former homeland. As noted above this song is said to have been written down in a letter, and not provided spontaneously on the spot like Tsangnyön's songs generally were according to his song-collection. This raises questions about how these songs were performed, composed, and disseminated.

In the song Tsangnyön gives the following instructions to Sönam Sangmo:

> See how death follows birth,
> since no one knows when death occurs,
> realize that it is urgent,
> and devote yourself to Dharma, day and night!
>
> See how that which has been constructed falls apart,
> abandon houses made of earth and stone,
> give up attachment to cities and farmland,
> and wander in remote mountains![207]

As seen in the excerpt, Tsangnyön encourages the noble lady to realize the impermanent nature of all phenomena and become a wandering *yoginī*. "If you want lasting happiness, escape the dungeons of *saṃsāra*! [...] If you want to leave the battle-fields of *saṃsāra*, defeat the armies of the enemy, self-clinging!",[208] he continues.

In this song, like in many of his other songs, the four thoughts that turn the mind [toward Dharma] (*blo zlog rnam bzhi*) figure prominently.[209] It is by realizing the value of the human life, the unfailing truth of impermanence, cause and result, and the

---

207 |*skyes nas 'chi ba mthong zhing* || *nam 'chi cha med yin pas* || *long med rgyud la bkal nas* || *nyin mtshan chos la 'bungs cig* (L: *shig*) || *rtsigs nas 'jig pa mthong bas* || *sa mkhar pe'u'i* (G: *spe'u'i*) *las dang* || *grong yul zhen pa bor la* (L: *spongs la*) || *gnyan sa ri khrod 'grims cig* (L: *shig*)|

208 *rgyun tu* (G; L: *du*) *bde zhing skyid par 'dod na* || *'khor ba'i btson* (G: *rtson*) *dong 'di las* (L: *la*) *bros cig* (G: *gcig*) | [...] |*'khor ba'i g.yul ngo zlog par 'dod na* || *bdag 'dzin dgra bo* (L: *dgra'o*) *dmangs su phob cig* (L: *shig*)|.

209 Many of Milarepa's songs also emphasizes the four thoughts.

shortcomings of cyclic existence, that the yogin realizes that the eight worldly concerns – striving for victory, fame, praise, and happiness, and avoiding defeat, obscurity, blame, and suffering – are utterly meaningless and should not concern the Buddhist yogin. Thus, the yogin ideally has a totally different way of thinking and acting, compared with a person concerned with worldly matters.

The second song with parting instructions appears on the front-side of page 13 of the song-collection.[210] There it is said that Tsangnyön, while staying in Gungtang (Gung thang), sent away his disciple Möndze Togden (Mon rdze rtogs ldan) to Kailash (Ti se), to "raise the victory banner of practice" (*sgrub pa'i rgyal mtshan 'dzugs*).

Before leaving, Möndze Togden requests instructions that would benefit him during his travelling and while practicing in Kailash. Tsangnyön then sang a song with parting instructions, containing advice for his yogin-disciple:

> Not abandoning worldly thoughts and deeds,
> while you have removed the outer signs of a worldly life
> and taken on the outer appearance of a monk
> – this is a fault that should be given up.
>
> Not being free from craving after wealth,
> even after having left behind one's homeland,
> and roaming the kingdoms aimlessly
> – this is a fault that should be given up.
>
> Being overpowered by desire for the eight worldly concerns,
> when you wander in remote mountains without companions,
> practicing asceticism and sustaining on water
> – this is a fault that should be given up.[211]

---

[210] This song is rendered in gTsang smyon, *gTsang pa he ru ka'i mgur 'bum*:13a–14b; G:101–104; L:60–63.

[211] *|'jig rten pa yi rtags* (G: *brags*) *bor nas* || *lus ser mo tsam du zhugs gyur kyang* || *bsam sbyor 'jig rten mi 'bor na* || *spang bar bya ba'i skyon mtshang* (G, L: *'tshang*) *yin* || *pha yul rgyab tu skyur nas ni* (G: *kyang*) || *rgyal khams phyogs med bskor lags kyang* || *zang zing gi 'dod pa ma bral* (G: *gral*) *na* || *'di yang spang bya'i* [÷] *'dra'o* (L: [...] *spang bya'i skyona'atshang yin*) || *grogs* (G: *grags*) *med ri khrod 'grim* (L: *'grims*) *bzhin* (G: *gzhin*) *du* || *dka' thub chu 'thung bgyis lags kyang* || *chos brgyad 'dod pas kun slang na* || *'di yang* [÷]|

Later in the same song, Tsangnyön provides Möndze Togden with several examples, showing him how to practice and how to live his life:

> When raising the victory-banner of practice,
> take the iron-peg, firmly driven into the ground, as an example,
> and practice with unshakable concentration!
>
> When roaming desolate mountains all alone,
> take the rhinoceros as an example,
> and practice without ever being tired or sad!
>
> When roaming the kingdoms aimlessly,
> take the feather, which is carried by the wind, as an example,
> and practice without clinging!
>
> When meeting with wealth and riches,
> take the food of a person who feels sick as an example,
> and practice without any desire or attachments![212]

These short excerpts demonstrate the ascetic and homeless ideal that Tsangnyön propagated, an ideal that had been upheld by Milarepa before him and effectively preached in Milarepa's songs. The same ascetic ideal also figures prominently in early Indian Buddhism. In the *Rhinoceros-Sūtra*, which is a very old Buddhist text preserved in Pali, Sanskrit, and Gandhari, it is mentioned that one should wander alone like the rhinoceros, for example.[213]

The third example of a song with parting instructions appears on the back-side of folio 20 of the song-collection.[214] When Tsangnyön was staying in the Crystal Cave in Nedum (Nas zlum shel phug), printing the collected works of Venerable Milarepa, he sang a song with parting instructions to his disciple Rinchen

---

212 *sgrub pa'i rgyal mtshan 'dzugs pa'i tshe* || *lcags phur spang la btab pa ltos* || *g.yo mgul* (G, L: *'gul*) *med pa nyams su long* || *gcig pur ri khrod 'grim pa'i tshe* || *ri dgas bse ru'i dpe la ltos* || *skyo ngal med par nyams su long* || *phyogs med rgyal khams bskor ba'i tshe* || *bya sgro rlung khyer dpe la ltos* || *zhen pa med par nyams su long* || *zang zing nor dang phrad pa'i* (G: *'phrad pa'i*) *tshe* || *skyug nad pa yi* (G: *pa'i*) *zas srid ltos* || *zhen chags med par nyams su long*|

213 Salomon 2000. See also Chapter 3 in this book.

214 This song is rendered in *gTsang smyon, gTsang pa he ru ka'i mgur 'bum*:20b–21a. The song is also rendered in G:143; L:99–100.

Palsangpo (Rin chen dpal bzang po), who was departing for Tsari (rTsa ri).[215] In this song, which I will render in full, Tsangnyön gives the following advice to his beloved disciple:

> Filled with devotion in body, speech, and mind,
> all the faithful sons in the knowledge-bearer's tradition
> bow down and praise,
> at the feet of the holy Kagyu (*bka' brgyud*) *lama*s.
>
> O Rinchenpal, you are like my heart!
> These are my heartfelt parting instructions.
> Do not forget them, keep them in your heart,
> think about them again and again!
>
> When you wander from place to place, aimlessly,
> transform the five objects that delight the senses to offerings.
> See through that which leads you astray,
> and let it, with caution, become the path!
>
> When Māra causes contrived respect to arise
> and your pride and selfishness increase,
> revert desire with determination in thoughts and actions!
>
> When you wander terrifying cemeteries
> and are haunted by the lord of the cemetery,
> realize that he is nothing else than your own mind!
>
> When you wander alone in isolated mountains
> and excellent experiences, good qualities,
> and the sign of warmth arise,
> realize this to be the kindness of the *lama*!
>
> When fortunate disciples gather around you,
> this is certainly due to karmic connections from before.
> Give them liberation and maturation
> by means of empowerments and instructions!
>
> When adverse circumstances and hindrances arise,
> these are my exhortations, urging you to engage in virtue.
> Be aware of this and pray to me again and again!

[215] Rinchen Palsangpo figures prominently in the song-collection and he is also depicted in it. The collection begins with a series of songs containing "pointing-out instructions" to Rinchen Palsangpo.

O son, you who are like my own heart!
Because of my great love for you,
I, your spiritual father, will always protect you.
Go now, meditate in the holy place Tsari!

May you meet with accomplishment, in thoughts and deeds,
in this and in your future lives!

Lamas, *yidams*, and protectors,
guard, and never be separated from, Rinchen Palsang!
May the teachings of the Kagyu spread!

Evaṃ![216]

This relatively short song enables us to get an idea of how Tsangnyön's songs are usually structured. Each song begins with an invocation to the *lama* and ends with the word *evaṃ*.[217] In-between there are instructions often directed to certain disciples,

---

[216] *|pha bka' rgyud bla ma dam pa'i zhabs la || dad ldan rigs 'dzin bu rgyud thams cad || sgo gsum gus pas phyag 'tshal bstod do || snying dang 'dra ba'i rin chen dpal la || 'gro chos snying gtam 'di skad smra bas || ma rjed snying la* (G, L: *sems la*) *yang yang bsoms cig* (L: *chongs cig*) *|| phyogs med rgyal khams 'grim pa'i tshe na || dbang po'i yul du 'dod yon rnam lngas || mchod par rdzus nas slu bar* (G: *glu bar*) *nges pas || khong zon drag pos lam du khyer cig || bdud kyis bzos pa'i* (L: *zos pa'i*) *bkur bsti* (G: *skur ti*) *byung tshe || nga rgyal rang 'dod je cher* (L: *che*) *'gro bas || zhen zlog* (G, L: *log*) *bsam sbyor drag po 'tshal lo || 'jigs rung dur khrod nyul ba'i tshe na || dur khrod bdag pos* (G: *bdag po'i*) *cho 'phrul yod bas* (G, L: *yong bas*) *|| rang gi sems su shes par gyis shig || gcig pur dben pa'i ri khrod 'grim tshe || nyams rtogs yon tan drod rtags skye bas || bla ma'i drin du shes par gyis cig* (L: *shig*) *|| skal ba ldan pa'i* (G: *skal bar ldan pa'i*) *bu slob 'dus na || sngon nas las 'brel yod par* (L: *yong bar*) *nges pas || dbang dang gdams pas* (L: *gdams pa*) *smin grol gyis cig || mi mthun rkyen ngan bar chad byung rung* (G: *tshe*) *|| kho bos dge sbyor bskul ba* (G: *skul ba*) (L: *kho bo dge la sbyor ba*) *yin pas || dran pas gsol ba yang yang thob cig || pha nga'i snying dang 'dra ba'i bu la || brtse ba chen pos 'bral med skyong gis || rtsa ri'i* (L: *tsa ri'i*) *gnas la* (G; L: *gangs la*) *sgom du song cig || skye dang tshe rabs 'di nyid du'ang* (L: *yang*) *|| bsam sbyor mthar phyin 'phrad par* (L: *phrad par*) *smon no || bla ma yi dam mkha' 'gro rnams kyis || rin chen dpal bzang 'bral med skyongs* (G: *skyong*) *shig* (G: *gcig*) *|| bka' rgyud bstan pa dar bar shog cig || e vaṃ||*

[217] This Indo-Aryan word, meaning something like 'this is how it is', marks the end of a song. According to Tibetan exegeses the two syllables express the final goal in Buddhism, the inseparability between emptiness (*e*) and method (*vaṃ*).

who usually are named in the narrative frame, which surrounds the song, and sometimes also in the song itself.

Let us now scrutinize the fourth song with parting instructions. This song begins on the front-side of folio 22 of the song-collection. It is rather long, spanning over several folios.[218] The song was performed/composed in Chuwar (Chu bar), a place situated not far from Lachi. Along with Kailash (Ti se) and Tsari, these were favoured places where Tsangnyön and his disciples spent much time practicing meditation. Chuwar is known as the place where Milarepa finally parted from this world and Tsangnyön spent much time in Chuwar during his later years. While Tsangnyön and his disciples were staying there, his disciple Chöchok Palsang (Chos mchog dpal bzang) decided to travel to Central Tibet to "practice for the benefit of others". Before he left, Tsangnyön sang a song with parting instructions, explaining how a person, who wants to achieve accomplishment, can get rid of the real enemy, namely ego-clinging (*bdag 'dzin*). Having introduced himself as a lazy person who wanders the cemeteries (*dur khrod nyul ba'i snyoms las pa*), Tsangnyön provides an exceptionally detailed account of how ego-clinging must be completely uprooted. Tsangnyön ends his song in the following manner:

With perseverance and without fear,
guard your *samaya*-commitments.
Refute and destroy the worldly way
and punish the enemy [– self-clinging –] according to the law as follows:

Catch it with the lasso of weariness and renunciation!
Fetter it with the iron chains of calm abiding and special insight!

Bring it to the court of justice of remote hermitages!
Sentence it by the truth of cause and effect!

Imprison it in the dungeon of stable meditation!
Flog it with the stick of post-meditation!

Cut off its feet that go after sense-pleasures!
Sever its hands that commit negative actions!

---

[218] This song is rendered in gTsang smyon, *gTsang pa he ru ka'i mgur 'bum*:22a–23b. Cf. G:166–169, not in L.

Put out its eyes that look after others' faults!
Detach its ears that listen to the impure mind!

Cut off its nose that smells the wind of unwholesome thoughts!
Pull out its tongue that praises oneself and disparages others!

Strip the skin off its body, which is hypocrisy!
Cut its life-vein, which is self-grasping!

[At the end,] when you have executed
your notorious mortal enemy in this way,
after having spent your former lives in beginningless *saṃsāra*,
discard also the rotten remains of the enemy
– self-grasping –
in the vast abyss, which is free from extremes!

Bury it in the earth, which is the fundamental likeness of *saṃsāra* and *nirvāṇa*!
Purify it in the water, which is to regard others as dearer than yourself!
Burn it in the fire of wisdom and knowledge!
Cast its ashes to the wind of *dharmatā*!

This is how you subdue the hated enemy – self-clinging.[219]

---

[219] |*'tsher med* (G: *'tshor med*) *dam tshig btson du* (G: *rtson du, my reading: brtson*) *zung* (G: *bzung*) || *phyi lam khegs pa'i* (G: *mkhag pa'i*) *rtsa ra dang* || *dgra lan khrims lugs 'di ltar gyis* || *skyo shas nges 'byung zhags pa khyigs* || *zhi lhag zung 'brel lcags sgrog chug* || *ri khrod dben pa'i khrims ra* (G: *pas*) *skor* || *rgyu 'bras bden pa'i khrims gtam thong* || *mnyam bzhag* (G: *gzhag*) *brtan po'i* (G: *btan po'i*) *brtson dong chug* || *rjes thob sgyu ma'i* (G: *rgyu ma'i*) *ber kas brdungs* (G: *bsdungs*) || *'dod yon rjes 'gro'i rkang pa bregs* (G: *grogs*) || *sdig las byed pa'i lag pa chod* (G: *grogs*) || *gzhan skyon lta ba'i mig 'bras thon* || *nyon mongs sgra* (G: *sbra* [?]) *nyan rna ba chod* || *ngan rtog rlung rgyu'i sna rtse bzhor* || *bdag bstod* (G: *stod*) *gzhan smod smra lce phyung* || *tshul 'chos* (G: *ches* [?]) *lus kyi lpags pa shus* (G: *gshus*) || *bdag tu 'dzin pa'i srog rtsa chod* || *de ltar gsad par gyur nas kyang* || *tshe rabs 'khor ba thog med nas* || *sha 'khon* (G: *khon*) *ha cang ches grags pas* || *bdag 'dzin dgra bo'i thed ro yang* || *mtha' bral chen po'i g.yang la skyur* || *srid zhi mnyam nyid sa la skungs* || *bdag pas gzhan gces chu la sbyongs* || *shes rab ye shes me la bsregs* || *thal ba chos nyid rlung la bskur* (G: *skur*) || *de bdag 'dzin sdang dgra'i* (G: … *'dzin dgra bo'i*) *'dul thabs yin*|

These four songs with parting instructions give us an idea about what Tsangnyön regarded to be important for travelling Buddhist yogins who wanted to attain the liberation from *saṃsāra*. The songs also illuminate the itinerant lifestyle that Tsangnyön followed and propagated.

III. Opening the Eyes of Faith

In 1503 Tsangnyön composed a catalogue about the history and function of songs. The catalogue is called *Opening the Eyes of Faith* and it was printed together with the song-collection and the above-mentioned catalogue listing its contents.[220] This text is particularly relevant to the present discussion because it contains Tsangnyön's own reflections about songs and their use. *Opening the Eyes of Faith* details the suitable forms such songs can take, their necessary elements, potential flaws, and beneficial effects. The text gives advice about how one should sing songs, to whom, and for what reasons.[221] Tsangnyön explains how the great *siddha*s of the past

> ... gave up clothes, food, and renown, and became the sons of mist and clouds. Wearing empty and secluded caves as their crowns [/hats], they cut the cord of happiness and abundance as aims of this life. They continuously remembered the difficulty of obtaining freedoms and advantages. For pillows they used mindfulness of the uncertainty of the time of death; for clothes they wore awareness of the infallibility of cause and effect; for mats they laid out mindfulness of *saṃsāra*'s shortcomings. Then, modelling themselves upon the downward descent of a river and the upward blaze of a lamp, they practiced the two stages of *yoga* continuously, day and night, without interruption. This resulted in the actualization of unmistaken experience and realization, which they then expressed in *vajra*-songs.[222]

---

[220] The full title of this work is *A Catalogue of Songs Dispelling the Darkness of Ignorance and Opening the Eyes of Faith* (*mGur gyi dkar chags ma rig mun sel dad pa'i mig 'byed*). The text is translated and analyzed in Larsson & Quintman 2015.

[221] Larsson and Quintman 2015:89.

[222] Larsson and Quintman 2015:97–98. gTsang smyon Heruka, *mGur gyi dkar chags*:1b: *sngon gyi rgyal ba grub thob gong ma rnams kyis dka' ba*

The catalogue is relatively short, spanning just 9 folios, and in it Tsangnyön encourages the catalogue's readers to sing songs and adopt the wandering and contemplative lifestyle of the early Kagyu yogins. If the singer of *mgur*

> is a yogin of the three sacred snow mountains, the outskirts of bustling towns, the middle reaches of slate and snow mountains, along the foothills of mist-shrouded woods, assembly halls where *vīra*s and *ḍākinī*s gather, the dwellings of noble sages, [such places are] the central mast of the great ship of the bKa' brgyud teachings, the cornerstone of the mansion of the Practice Lineage teaching, a great sacred site where meditation naturally increases.[223]

Tsangnyön is here speaking to those yogins who wander among "the three sacred snow-mountains", a reference to the great pilgrimage mountains of Kailash, Lachi, and Tsari, each of which had become an important Kagyu retreat-site by the late 15th century.[224]

Tsangnyön concludes his catalogue about songs with a short reflection on the value of *mgur* and how wandering yogins like himself and his followers might employ Buddhist songs of experience in a practical way. The songs are

---

dang du blangs | theg pa khur du khur| dman pa'i sa bzung | hrul po'i gos gyon | rgyan cha sems la btags | gyong lto gos gtam gsum la btang | sprin dang na bun gyi bu byas | mi med kyi brag phug stong pa rnams zhwa ltar du gyon nas | tshe 'di'i 'dun ma bde skyid phun tshogs la re thag gcad te | dal 'byor rnyed par dka' ba rgyun chags su yid la bsams | nam 'chi nges med dran pa rngas su bcug | rgyu 'bras blu (bslu) med dran pa gos su gyon | 'khor ba'i nyes dmigs dran pa gdan du bting nas | chu bo thur du 'bab pa'am | mar me gyen du 'bar ba dper bzhag ste | nyin mtshan khor yug tu rgyun chad med par rim gnyis kyi rnal 'byor nyams su blangs pa'i don 'bras | nyams dang rtogs pa phyin ci ma log pa sngon (mngon) du gyur nas rdo rje'i mgur gsungs pa rnams lags shing |.

223 Larsson & Quintman 2015:107. gTsang smyon Heruka, *mGur gyi dkar chags*:8b: *gnas gsum gangs ri'i rnal 'byor pa yin na | 'du 'dzi grong gi pha rol | g.ya' dang gangs kyi nang khongs | nags dang na bun 'khrigs pa'i 'dabs rol | dpa' bo mkha' 'gro 'du ba'i tshogs khang | drang srong 'phags pa bzhugs pa'i sti gnas | bka' rgyud bstan pa'i gru chen gzhung shing || sgrub rgyud bstan pa'i khang bzangs (bzang) rmangs brdo (rmang rdo) | bsam gtan ngang gis 'phel ba'i gnas chen |.*

224 Larsson and Quintman 2015:107.

> provisions when wandering in charnel grounds and holy places, necessities when roaming savage lands and mountain retreats, offerings when meeting *lamas*, gifts when encountering *dharma* brothers, offering articles when visiting temples and *stūpas*, goods when travelling around the countryside, ferry-fees when crossing rivers, offering gifts for requests to kings, an axe for chipping away [alms from] the wealthy and a file for scraping away [alms] from the poor. Even when meeting bandits we reply in song, and on such occasions the advice should be an exhortation to practice virtue.[225]

In Tsangnyön's view, *mgur* thus serve not just as spontaneous records of awakened experience attained by great masters of the past; rather, they retain a material relevance in the world that lies beyond their soteriological value. For the yogin with few material possessions, *mgur* function as transactional objects of great practical value. Songs become a form of religious capital that may be given as gifts to *lamas* and fellow practitioners. They may serve as fees for ferrymen when crossing rivers, they may be presented as tribute to kings, they may be used to garner offerings from the rich and the poor alike. Songs may even be exploited to save one's own skin in the event of attack by bandits.[226]

IV. Concluding remarks

Let us leave Tsangyön's catalogue about songs and return to his collected songs. The song-collection ends with Tsangnyön's final words. These words were obviously seen as especially important, since they are cited in two of the three extant hagiographies about him, as well as in a hagiography about his biographer Ngödrub Pembar (dNgos grub dpal 'bar).[227]

---

[225] Larsson & Quintman 2015:127. gTsang smyon Heruka, *mGur gyi dkar chags*:8b: *gnas chen dang dur khrod myul ba'i 'tsho chas | snyan sa (gnyan sa) ri khrod 'grim pa'i yo byad | bla ma la 'jal (mjal) ba'i phyag rten | mched grogs dang 'jal ba'i skyes ka (kha) | lha khang mchod rten 'jal ba'i mchod rdzas | rgyal khams skor ba'i yang zong | chu rab sgrol ba'i gru rdzas | rgyal po la zhu ba'i zhu sten (rten) | phyug po la bzhog pa'i sta gri | dbul po la 'brad pa'i se gdar | ar ba (pa) phyag (jag) pa dang 'phrad kyang dbyangs su tsher re len pa lags pas | da lan 'dir yang gsung sgros la dge ba'i bskul ma |.*

[226] Larsson and Quintman 2015:106.

[227] dNgos grub dpal 'bar (1456–1527), *Dad pa'i seng ge*: 26b; rGod tshang

Before he passed away, Tsangnyön said:

> Monks, disciples, and patrons, since you have met Milarepa himself in these degenerate times, you have fortunate *karma*. Continue to study the liberation story of Mila and devote your entire life to practice! Then you will hear [my] real speech, and you will be taken care of.[228]

These words are often cited by Tsangnyön's disciples as one of several indications proving that Tsangnyön was Milarepa incarnate; Tsangnyön here reveals his true identity. The yogin *par excellence* had reappeared after some four hundred years for the sake of continuing his previous mission. This time Milarepa appeared in disguise of a crazy yogin, who devoted his life to re-establish the wandering yogic lifestyle of Milarepa, a lifestyle that had become increasingly rare, even in the very lineage that Milarepa followed – the Kagyu lineage.[229]

According to the sources that portray Tsangnyön and his disciples, they practiced the same teachings and lived the same lifestyle as Milarepa had done, alternating between meditation-practice in isolated places and homeless wandering. Moreover, they collected the aural teachings (*snyan brgyud*), the liberation-accounts (*rnam thar*), and the songs (*mgur*) of the early Kagyu masters, including Milarepa's, which they printed and spread.[230] Besides making the songs and hagiographies of the previous masters in their tradition available, they also composed and printed hagiographies and songs about their personal masters and composed their own songs, which they also printed and spread. In this way, by various means, they effectively presented a yogic alternative to the monastic lifestyle that had increasingly become favoured

ras pa, *Nyi ma'i snying po*:273; Byams pa lha btsun grags pa, *Paṇ chen gzhung brgya pa'i rnam thar*:11.

[228] gTsang smyon, *gTsang pa he ru ka'i mgur 'bum*:27a: *grwa pa bu slob yon bdag dang bcas pa rnams | snyigs dus mi la ras pa dang dngos su 'jal ba yin pas | las dang skal pa bzang | da dung mi la'i rnam thar la ltos la | tshe dang sgrub pa snyoms | dngos su gsung thos par 'gyur zhing rjes su 'dzin no* | For alternative English translations, see Quintman 2006:260; Larsson 2012:187; Stearns [Kalnins] 1985:81.

[229] Cf. Smith 2001: 60.

[230] Cf. Schaeffer 2009; Schaeffer 2011; Sernesi 2011a; Sernesi 2011b.

for a person who wanted to engage seriously in Buddhist practice in 15th century Tibet. Tsangnyön and his disciples claimed that it was still possible to wander alone like a rhinoceros, just like Milarepa and the early Kagyu yogins supposedly had done some hundreds of years earlier. At the same time, they were following the ancient path of some of the early, ascetically inclined Buddhist monks of India,[231] trying to bring new life into a very old lifestyle. Tsangnyön and his disciples proved that this way of life was not merely an ancient ideal to read and hear about, but a lifestyle to be emulated by apt yogins. They showed this both by personal example and by textual production, thus making their message extraordinarily trustworthy and powerful.

These wandering yogins and *yoginīs*[232] apparently identified so thoroughly with masters who had lived earlier, that subject and object sometimes fused and became one. According to the hagiographies written about them, the statues and preserved blockprint illustrations that depict them – and, indeed, according to their songs as well – they literally lived in the footsteps of their forebears, dressed like them, practiced the same religious practices, meditated in the same caves, walked the same paths, and so forth. Thus, they seem to have led their lives in accordance with biographical patterns, which they themselves actively promoted and sometimes even created.[233] By expressing themselves through religious poetry (*mgur*), which they created themselves, instead of via translated canonical texts, these yogins could present Buddhism in an innovative way that was adapted to their audience's needs. In doing so they skilfully presented an alternative way of practicing Buddhism, outside of the monasteries. They claimed that it was not necessary to be a monk and live in a monastery in order to attain insight and awakening. The path of the wandering yogin was open to men and women, monks and lay-people, but the

---

[231] See Chapter 3 in this book.

[232] Tsangnyön had many female followers and by appointing Kuntu Sangmo (Kun tu bzang mo, 1464–1549) as his successor, just before his death, he showed that it was possible for a woman to attain the highest possible position in his lineage.

[233] There are some interesting parallels with the way in which Tsangnyön and his disciples followed in the footsteps of their forebears and Thomas Mann's notion "a life in quotation". Cf. Jan Assmann (2006:155–177).

path required a great deal of fortitude and devotion. The path of the wandering yogin that they outlined was not a novel innovation, but an ancient ideal that existed in early Buddhism, and indeed, also before Buddhism arose in various contexts and times.

It is noteworthy that various layers of textual interactions are demonstrated in these songs. Julia Kristeva writes about three dimensions of dialogue that needs to be considered when studying a text: the writing subject, addressee, and the exterior text itself.[234] The meaning of a text can only be fully understood in relation to other texts and contexts. Therefore, the intertextual relationships within the textual *corpus* in which the songs are found, and the specific Buddhist tradition to which they belong, as well as the historical, political, and social contexts, need to be taken into consideration when trying to understand these songs. It is important to widen the contexts around the songs, to involve other than merely intertextual aspects: we should reconsider the way in which texts and lives interplay, and recognize the people who created the texts and sang the songs, as well as the people who listened to them and used them in different ways. When it comes to understanding the role and function of these figures and traditions, literary and otherwise, the concept of "liminality" and "communitas", as outlined by the anthropologist Victor Turner, could be utilized.[235] The Tibetan yogins who sang the songs and compiled and printed the texts containing the songs appears to have lived in what Turner calls a state of "liminality", and in "communitas of withdrawal and retreat".[236]

I also believe that the Russian philosopher and literary theorist Michail Bakhtin's ground-breaking study of humour and culture in the European Middle Ages and the Renaissance can help us comprehend the Tibetan texts and contexts more accurately. Bakhtin explores how the carnival, as depicted in the novels of François Rabelais – a contemporary of Tsangnyön and his disciples – with its emphasis on the earthy and the grotesque, signified the symbolic destruction of authority and official culture and the

[234] Kristeva 1980:66.
[235] Turner 1995 [1969].
[236] Turner 1995 [1969]:154.

assertion of popular renewal.[237] The official and non-official are in constant dialogue with one another. To fully understand the official (institutionalized) monastic forms of Buddhism in Tibet, one must consider the non-official (non-monastic) forms of Buddhism. The work of both Bakhtin and Rabelais springs from an age of revolution, and each reflects a particularly open sense of the literary text.

It is noteworthy that Tibet in the 15th and 16th centuries experienced rapid transitions and change. It is also striking that the creators of the songs, which this chapter focuses on, were closer to the popular tradition of Tibet than the learned monks and the more scholastic texts. In general, the creators of the songs lived outside of the monasteries and their songs and hagiographies are "distinguished from many other, quite boring and pedantic, works by their near-colloquial language, their lively style, and above all the interest they take in countless details of real life."[238] According to Rolf Stein it is their creators' communion "with popular sources of inspiration that made them the greatest creators of Tibetan literature".[239] I believe that it is crucial for our understanding of these songs and their compilers to examine the full contexts around them, popular as well as learned. People and texts were in a dialogic and intertextual relationship with other people and other texts. There is also a reciprocal relationship between celibate monks, who live in monasteries, and non-celibate yogins, who live in caves and wander, as well as between hagiographies and songs, on one hand, and the scholastic works, on the other.

References

Tibetan texts

Byams pa lha btsun grags pa. 2005. *Paṇ chen gzhung brgya pa'i rnam thar*. Full title: *Dpal ldan bla ma dam pa gzhung brgya smra ba'i seng ge siddhi'i mtshan can gyi rnam par thar pa yon tan gyi rgya mtsho la dad pa'i rba rlabs rnam par g.yo ba*. Hong Kong: Shang kang than mā.

Don grub rgyal (1953–1985). 1997. "Bod kyi mgur glu byung 'phel gyi lo rgyus dang khyad chos bsdus par ston pa rig pa'i khye'u

237 Bakhtin 1984 [1965].

238 Stein 1995 [1972]:276.

239 Stein 1995 [1972]:276.

rnam par rtsen pa'i skyed tshal." In: *Dpal don grub rgyal gyi gsung 'bum*. Vol. 3, 316–601. Beijing: Mi rigs dpe skrun khang.

rGod tshang ras pa (1482–1559). *dKar chags nyi 'od snang ba*. Sammlung Waddell. Wadd 120 h. Folio 9b–10b. Staatsbibliothek zu Berlin – Preussischer Kulturbesitz, Orientabteilung.

——— *Nyi ma'i snying po*. Abbreviated as G in the footnotes. Full title: *gTsang smyon he ru ka phyogs thams cad las rnam par rgyal ba'i rnam thar rdo rje theg pa'i gsal byed nyi ma'i snying po*. Published as *The Life of the Saint of Gtsang*. New Delhi: Śatapiṭaka Series, vol. 69. Edited by Lokesh Chandra. Preface by Gene E. Smith. New Delhi: Sharada Rani. 1969. TBRC, W4CZ1247. Printed in 1512.

lHa btsun rin chen rnam rgyal (1473–1557). *Dad pa'i spu slong g.yo ba*. Abbreviated as L in the footnotes. Full title: *Grub thob gtsang pa smyon pa'i rnam thar dad pa'i spu slong g.yo ba*. In: *Bde mchog mkha' 'gro snyan rgyud (Ras chung snyan rgyud): Two manuscript collections of texts from the yig cha of Gtsang-smyon He-ru-ka*, vol. 1. Edited by S.W. Tashi gang pa, 1–129. Leh: Smanrtsis shesrig spendzod. 1971. Printed in 1543.

dNgos grub dpal 'bar (1456–1527). *Dad pa'i seng ge. rJe btsun gtsang pa he ru ka'i thun mong gi rnam thar yon tan gyi gangs ril dad pa'i seng ge rnam par rtse ba*. NGMPP reel L834/2. TBRC, W2CZ6647. Printed in 1508.

gTsang smyon Heruka (1452–1507). *mGur gyi dkar chags. mGur gyi dkar chags ma rig mun sel dad pa'i mig 'byed*. Xylograph in the collection of Sammlung Waddell. Wadd 120 h. Staatsbibliothek zu Berlin – Preussischer Kulturbesitz, Orientabteilung. Printed in 1503.

——— *gTsang pa he ru ka'i mgur 'bum. rJe btsun gtsang pa he ru ka'i mgur 'bum rin po che dbang gi rgyal po thams cad mkhyen pa'i lam ston*. Edited by rGod tshang ras pa *et alii*. NGMPP reel L567/2. TBRC, W4CZ1248.

Literature in other languages

Ardussi, John Albert. 1977. "Brewing and Drinking the Beer of Enlightenment in Tibetan Buddhism: The Dohā Tradition in Tibet". In: *Journal of the American Oriental Society* 97(2), 115–124.

Assmann, Jan. 2006. *Religion and Cultural Memory: Ten Studies*. Translated by Rodney Livingstone. Stanford, Calif.: Stanford University Press.

Bakhtin, M. M. 1981 [1930s]. *The Dialogic Imagination: Four Essays*. Edited by Michael Holquist. Translated by Caryl Emerson and Michael Holquist. Austin and London: University of Texas Press.

——— 1984 [1965]. *Rabelais and His World*. Translated by Hélène Iswolsky. Bloomington IN: Indiana University Press.

Braitstein, Lara. 2014. *The Adamantine Songs (Vajragīti): Study, Translation, and Tibetan Critical Edition*. New York: American Institute of Buddhist Studies.

Chang, Garma C.C. (trans.). 1989 [1962]. *The Hundred Thousand Songs of Milarepa*. Boston: Shambhala Publications.

DiValerio. 2015. "Reanimating the Great Yogin: On the Composition of the Biographies of the Madman of Tsang (1452–1507)". In: *Revue d'Etudes Tibétaines* 32, 25–49.

Ehrhard, Franz-Karl. 2010. "Editing and Publishing the Master's Writings: The Early Years of rGod tshang ras chen (1482–1559)." In: *Edition, éditions: l'écrit au Tibet, évolution et devenir*, (Collectanea Himalayica, 3). Edited by A. Chayet, C. Scherrer-Schaub, F. Robin & J. L. Achard, 129–161. München: Indus Verlag.

Evans-Wentz, Walter (ed.). 2000 [1928]. *Tibet's Great Yogi Milarepa: A Biography from the Tibetan*. Translated by Lama Kazi Dawa-Samdup. Oxford: Oxford University Press.

Guenther, Herbert V. 1969. *The Royal Songs of Saraha: A Study in the History of Buddhist Thought*. Seattle: University of Washington Press.

Jackson, Roger R. 1996. "'Poetry' in Tibet: Glu, mGur, sNyan ngag and 'Songs of Experience'". In: *Tibetan Literature: Studies in Genre*. Edited by J. I. Cabezón & R. R. Jackson, 368–392. Ithaca, New York: Snow Lion Publications.

——— 2004. *Tantric Treasures: Three Collections of Mystical Verse from Buddhist India*. New York: Oxford University Press.

Jinpa, Thupten & Jaś Elsner (trans.). 2000. *Songs of Spiritual Experience: Tibetan Buddhist Poems of Insight and Awakening*. Boston: Shambhala Publications.

Jong, J. W. de 1959. *Mi la ras pa'i rnam thar: Texte tibétain de la vie de Milarépa*. Haag: Mouton.

Kapstein, Matthew T. 2006. "An Inexhaustible Treasury of Verse: The Literary Legacy of the Mahāsiddhas". In: *Holy Madness: Portraits of Tantric Siddhas*. Edited by R. Linrothe, 49–62. Chicago: Serindia Publications.

Kristeva, Julia. 1980. *Desire in Language: A Semiotic Approach to Literature and Art*. Edited by Leon S. Roudiez. Translated by Thomas Gora. Oxford: Blackwell.

Kunga Rinpoche, and Brian Cutillo (trans.). 1986. *Miraculous Journey: New Stories and Songs by Milarepa*. Novato: Lotsawa.

——— 1995 [1978]. *Drinking the Mountain Stream: Song of Tibet's Beloved Saint, Milarepa*. Boston: Wisdom Publications.

Kværne, Per. 1977. *An Anthology of Buddhist Tantric Songs*. Oslo: Universitetsforlaget.

Larsson, Stefan. 2012. *Crazy for Wisdom: The Making of a Mad Yogin in Fifteenth-Century Tibet*. Leiden: Brill.

——— 2016. "Prints about the Printer: Four Early Prints in Honour of the Mad Yogin of gTsang". In: *Tibetan Printing: Comparison, Continuities, and Change*. Edited by H. Diemberger, F-K. Ehrhard & P. Kornicki, 309–331. Leiden: Brill.

——— 2018. *Tsangnyön Herukas sånger: En studie och översättning av en tibetansk buddhistisk yogis religiösa poesi*. Lund: Nordic Academic Press.

——— 2019a. "The Crazy yogis of Tibet". In: *Brill's Encyclopedia of Buddhism*. Leiden: Brill.

——— 2019b. "Gtsang smyon Heruka". In: *Brill's Encyclopedia of Buddhism*. Leiden: Brill.

Larsson, Stefan & Andrew Quintman. 2015. "Opening the Eyes of Faith: Constructing Tradition in a Sixteenth-Century Catalogue of Tibetan Religious Poetry". In: *Revue d'Etudes Tibétaines* 32, 87–151.

Lhalungpa, Lobsang P. (trans.). 1979 [1977]. *The Life of Milarepa*. New York: Arkana.

Nālandā Translation Committee (trans.). 1986. *The Life of Marpa the Translator*. Boston: Shambhala Publications.

——— (trans.). 1989. *The Rain of Wisdom*. Boston: Shambhala Publications.

Quintman, Andrew. 2014. *The Yogin and the Madman: Reading the Biographical Corpus of Tibet's Great Saint Milarepa*. New York: Columbia University Press.

Ruegg, David Seyfort. 1997. "The Preceptor-Donor (yon mchod) Relation in Thirteenth Century Tibetan Society and Polity, its Inner Asian Precursors and Indian Models". In: *Tibetan Studies: Proceedings of the 7th Seminar of the International Association for Tibetan Studies, 1995*. 857–872. Vienna: Verlag der Österreichischen Akademie der Wissenschaften.

Salomon, Richard. 2000. *A Gāndhārī Version of the Rhinoceros Sūtra*. Seattle: University of Washington Press.

Schaeffer, Kurtis R. 2005. *Dreaming the Great Brahmin: Tibetan Traditions of the Buddhist Poet-Saint Saraha*. New York: Oxford University Press.

——— 2009. *The Culture of the Book in Tibet*. New York: Columbia University Press.

——— 2011. "The Printing Projects of gTsang smyon Heruka and his Disciples". In: *Mahāmudrā and the bKa'-brgyud Tradition. PIATS 2006. Tibetan Studies: Proceedings of the 11th Seminar of the International Association for Tibetan Studies, Königswinter 2006*. Ed. by R. Jackson & M. Kapstein, 453–479. Halle (Saale): International Institute for Tibetan and Buddhist Studies.

Sernesi, Marta. 2011a. "A Continuous Stream of Merit: The Early Reprints of gTsang smyon Heruka's Hagiographical Works". In: *Zentral Asiatische Studien* 40, 179–237.

——— 2011b. "The Aural Transmission of Saṃvara: An Introduction to Neglected Sources for the Study of the Early bKa' brgyud".

In: *Mahāmudrā and the bKa'-brgyud Tradition. PIATS 2006: Tibetan Studies: Proceedings of the 11th Seminar of the International Association for Tibetan Studies, Königswinter 2006*. Ed. by R. Jackson & M. Kapstein, 179–209. Halle (Saale): International Institute for Tibetan and Buddhist Studies.

Smith, E. Gene. 2001. *Among Tibetan Texts: History and Literature of the Himalayan Plateau*. Edited by Kurtis R. Schaeffer. Boston: Wisdom Publications.

Stearns, Cyrus Rembert. 2000. *The Hermit of Go Cliffs: Timeless Instructions from a Tibetan Mystic*. Boston: Wisdom Publications.

——— 2012. *Songs of the Road: The Poetic Travel of Tsarchen Losal Gyatso*. Boston: Wisdom Publications.

Stearns [Kalnins], Ilze Maruta. 1985. The Life of Gtsang smyon Heruka: A Study of Divine Madness. Master's Thesis, University of Washington.

Stein, Rolf Auriel. 1988 [1972]. *Tibetan Civilization*. California: Stanford University Press.

Sujata, Victoria. 2005. *Tibetan Songs of Realization: Echoes from a Seventeenth-Century Scholar and Siddha in Amdo*. Leiden: Brill.

——— 2012. *Songs of Shabkar: The Path of a Tibetan Yogi Inspired by Nature*. Berkeley: Dharma Publishing.

Sørensen, Per K. 1990. *Divinity Secularized: An Enquiry into the Nature and Form of the Songs Ascribed to the Sixth Dalai Lama*. Vienna: Arbeitskreis für Tibetische und Buddhistische Studien, Universität Wien.

Templeman, David. 1994. "Dohā, Vajragīti and Caryā Songs". In: *Tantra and Popular Religion in Tibet*. Edited by G. Samuel, H. Gregor & E. Stutchbury, 15–38. New Delhi: Aditya.

Tsangnyön Heruka. 2010 [1488]. *The Life of Milarepa*. Translated by A. Quintman. New York: Penguin Books.

——— 2017. *The Hundred Thousand Songs of Milarepa*. Translated by C. Stagg. Boulder: Shambhala Publications.

Turner, Victor. 1995 [1969]. *The Ritual Process: Structure and Anti-structure*. New York: Aldine De Gruyter.

Yamamoto, Carl. 2015. "A Preliminary Survey of the Songs of Zhang Tshal pa". In: *The Illuminating Mirror: Tibetan Studies in Honour of Per K. Sørensen on the Occasion of his 65th Birthday*. Edited by O. Czaja & G. Hazod, 541–578. Wiesbaden: Ludwig Reichert Verlag.

5. Spiritual Localization and De-localization: Traditional and Modern Patterns in Hindu Pilgrimage

Heinz Werner Wessler

Abstract

Going on pilgrimage is a vivid tradition in India and its masterpieçe, the Kumbh Mela, is probably the biggest mega-event of its kind in the world. The identification of holy places at established places of pilgrimage is an ongoing process even in our times, contributing to the diffusion-mechanisms of certain pilgrimages. In contradiction to this, the criticism of the institution of pilgrimage has formed an important stream for centuries. The monistic tradition in Hinduism has produced many popular poems that question the reward of religious journeying and ritual bathing at holy places, or that transform pilgrimage into a metaphor for inner journeys towards liberation.

I. Introduction

Numerous places all over on the map of South Asia attract millions of Hindu pilgrims every year. Some of them draw predominantly regional pilgrims,[240] others draw pilgrims from all over India. Some traditional places are on the decline, others are gaining in

[240] Compare for example the many pilgrimage-sites in the Central Himalayas in Datar 1961 and Berreman 1963.

How to cite this book chapter:
Wessler, H. W. 2021. Spiritual Localization and De-localization: Traditional and Modern Patterns in Hindu Pilgrimage. In: Larsson, S. and af Edholm, K. (eds.) *Songs on the Road: Wandering Religious Poets in India, Tibet, and Japan*. Pp. 93–112. Stockholm: Stockholm University Press. DOI: https://doi.org/10.16993/bbi.e.

importance, like the pilgrimage to Amarnath in Kaśmīr, which together with its religious meaning also has a political meaning, since it marks Kaśmīr as a part of the holistic setup of Indian national territory.[241] The ranking is flexible, and new places come up, often together with upcoming school-traditions that draft their own religious landscape and mark sacred places, as for example the pilgrimage to the temples of the Swāmīnārāyaṇs or to the Sai Baba of Śirdī that go back to charismatic founders or new formations in the 19th and early 20th century. Large-scale road construction work is going on at many places, as for example along the upper Gaṅgā to the pilgrimage places in the Central Himālayas. Bhadrināth, Gaṅgotrī, and other places that are high up in the mountains, are more and more easily accessible by car and bus, and even by helicopter.[242] Walking pilgrims, expecting a better reward for the trouble, are still visible, but modern transportation has radically changed the nature of pilgrimage overall. Easy accessibility has become important for the great majority of religious travellers.

Religious pilgrimage (*tīrthayātrā*), and particularly Hindu pilgrimage, is blossoming in contemporary India probably like never before. Many traditional texts like the epics and the *Purāṇas* have long sections on rewards for certain pilgrimages (*phalastuti*). The *phalastuti* very often forms an integral part of religious narrative texts, particularly those directly or indirectly related to certain places of pilgrimage (*sthalapurāṇas*).[243] These texts are mostly in the classical holy language of Hinduism, that is Sanskrit, sometimes transmitted as independent texts, but are often included in larger canonical works, mostly epics and *Purāṇas*. The *phalastuti* often refers explicitly to the trias of *yātrā* (travel), *darśana* (seeing the divine image/symbol), and *snāna* (purification in water) that define the common essential of pilgrimage.[244] They are often accompanied by other activities like *muṇḍana* (ritual head-shaving),

---

241 www.jammu.com/shri-amarnath-yatra/schedule.php (19.1.2019)

242 A regular helicopter service is offered for one day pilgrimages from Dehradun to Bhadrināth, compare: chardhampackage.com/badrinath-yatra-by-helicopter.html (19.1.2019)

243 Compare Bhardwaj 1973:153, 216–224 for a case study of text sources on Haridwar. Compare also the nine case studies in Bakker 1990.

244 Bhardwaj 1973:153.

piṇḍadāna (sacrifice of rice-balls to the ancestors), investiture of the holy thread, and other rituals.

Singh, who has published on Banaras as a centre of Hindu pilgrimage for decades, describes the overall function of pilgrimage as "deeper interconnectedness",[245] and the landscape of the place of pilgrimage as "sacredscape". These trendy abstractions may be attractive for Western observers or eventually researchers, but they are – in English original or some kind of translation into Indian languages – quite far away from the reference-frames of the great majority of the pilgrims. In any case, the circulation-mechanism through pilgrimage has certainly contributed a lot to the identity of Hinduism as a conclusive whole[246] and it still fulfils this function in contemporary India.

Besides, while in colonial India, and even in the decades after independence, pilgrimage was largely perceived as a kind of inferior form of performing Hinduism, it has somehow entered the centre-stage in the meantime. The recent holy dip at the central place of the 2019 Kumbh Mela in Prayagraj (Allahabad) of the chief minister of the state of Uttar Pradesh, Yogi Adityanath (BJP), together with a group of members of his cabinet, was covered by the media all over India.[247] Following this media event, oppositional Congress Party leaders, including Priyanka and Rahul Gandhi, also started to decide going for the holy dip.[248] This recent development demonstrates how pilgrimage has political dimensions and political functions, particularly in contemporary discourses on identity-politics in India.

At the same time, traditional as well as modern Hinduism has produced manifest forms of criticism of the institution of pilgrimage and religious journeying as such and can even be explicitly polemical. Besides, textual sources for pilgrimages have sometimes a metaphorical meaning and are not necessarily meant

[245] Compare Feldhaus 2003.

[246] Glasenapp 1928; Bhardwaj 1985; Feldhaus 2003.

[247] Compare: www.indiatoday.in/india/story/yogi-adityanath-does-a-har-har-gange-takes-dip-during-kumbh-mela-at-prayagraj-1441808-2019-01-29 (30.1.2019)

[248] www.indiatoday.in/india/story/priyanka-gandhi-may-begin-political-innings-with-holy-dip-at-kumbh-1439977-2019-01-26 (1.2.2019)

literally. For example, a Yogi can perform a pilgrimage to the seven shrines in meditation, without any physical move.[249]

II. The pilgrim and the tourist

A Google-search after places of pilgrimage in India quickly reveals a certain canon of places – mostly Hindu, but some Muslim or possibly other religions. Most of these websites are designed for the growing market of tourists who would like to observe and to a certain degree participate in religious life that is not the religious life of their own.[250] Titles like "Best pilgrimage and religious sites in India"[251] clearly appeal to the grey zone between observation and participation. While "Visit Dargah Sharif" points more to the tourist as observer – perhaps not by chance a Muslim pilgrimage-centre – "Take a boat ride" in the artificial lake in the recently constructed gigantic Akshardham temple-compound in Delhi goes a step further from tourism to pilgrimage. "Engage in a trek to the Amarnath Caves" maintains the ambiguity between trekking and pilgrimage that seems to be part of the marketing strategy, while "Take part in the Holla Mohalla" (Sikh festival) and "Take a holy dip" point to performative, participatory activities.

"Tour packages" that include a certain, though limited, participation in religious festivals are common. Some sites operate freely with self-affirmative statements like "In India we find oldest pilgrimage tradition in the whole world"[252], "You can find numerous temple towns, exotic pilgrimage sites and unique rituals in the country"[253], or commonplaces like "India is a land of spirituality"[254]. They invite to book "spiritual tour packages" focused on the visit of old and modern centres of pilgrimages, *et cetera*. The great majority of these websites focus on international tourists. The emphasis on experience in touristic discourse aligns tourism

---

249 Bharati 1963.

250 Jacobsen 2009:407f.

251 www.indianholiday.com/best-of-india/pilgrimage-religious (19.1.2019)

252 Compare: www.culturalindia.net/indian-pilgrimage (19.1.2019)

253 www.travelogyindia.com/pilgrimage-tours (19.1.2019)

254 www.hindustantimes.com/india-news/a-record-over-24-crore-people-visited-kumbh-2019-more-than-total-tourists-in-up-in-2014-17/story-9uncpmhBPnBj11ClnTiYQP.html (6.10.2020)

with religion in the modern world in general and with the focus on religious experience in modern Hinduism in particular.[255]

The discovery of traditional places of pilgrimage by the tourism-industry is part of the dynamics of contemporary tourism. Naturally, it leaves hardly any space for the complicated debates on religious merits of religious travelling to certain places or of pilgrimage in general, on how meaning is created, reinforced, and maintained through pilgrimage. It supports a view that religious identities are substantial, fixed, and unchanging. Tourism is sympathetic and affirmative to pilgrimage. It questions the identity of the pilgrim more implicit than explicit by exposing her or him to the observant view from outside that the tourist persistently maintains even if she or he participates to a certain extent.

Besides, the Hindu pilgrim and the national or international tourist have much in common. They both take photographs of themselves together with landmarks of the pilgrimage-place, sometimes in devotional postures. They both are interested in purchasing souvenirs and gifts, and they avail themselves of the same transportation and sometimes lodging accommodations. Tourists visiting Hindu temples and pilgrimage-sites often participate in religious rites, sometimes under the pressure of temple-priests (in expectation of a certain amount of money as reward for their services), out of curiosity or eventually because they are overtaken by religious sensations and a sense of participation in religious rituals. Religious pilgrims are often interested in visiting non-religious places while on pilgrimage.[256] In other words, the binary of "outer journey" and "inner journey", which is also part of the traditional criticism of pilgrimage within the Hindu tradition, is always blurred.[257] Overall, tourism to pilgrimage-places and festivals related to pilgrimages do not appear to have a destabilizing effect on the tradition of Hindu pilgrimage, but rather complement its attraction and affirm it.

The biggest, and most spectacular, religious pilgrimage of India and the world, is the Kumbh Mela. It takes place every three years at four different places (Allahabad, Haridwar, Ujjain, and Nasik)

---

[255] Compare Bremer 2005; Singh 2006.

[256] Bremer 2005.

[257] Singh 2006 strongly emphasizes touring and pilgrimage as a binary.

and the festival at the confluence of the rivers Gaṅgā and Yamunā – plus the mythical Sarasvatī – is the most important place of the Kumbh Mela. The confluence of the three rivers (*triveṇī*) is perceived as a holy site and place of pilgrimage any time, but the Kumbh Mela is believed to be the most auspicious time to visit it. Pilgrims come from across India in millions: simple farmers and their families, businessmen, whole villages, and the picturesque "holy men", *sādhus* from all over India. The recent Ardh Kumbh Mela in Prajagraj (Allahabad) had to deal with an incredible number of nearly 250 million visitors according to news reports. In other words, an extreme form of mass mobilization within the rather narrow time-frame of only a few weeks, between Makar Sankranti on January 15th and Shivratri on March 4th 2019. Among the visitors were supposedly more than one million foreign nationals, mostly tourists in the strict sense of the term. Tents were set up in an area of about 24 square kilometres at the holy site, an incredible number of 122000 mobile toilets and drainage systems, dozens of pontoon bridges over the rivers, 150 kilometres of newly constructed roads, electricity-grids, hundreds of new bus stations and even several provisional hospitals. Beyond the central planning, more than 5000 more or less self-organized mobile *āśrams* were set up by the many Hindu religious orders that participated, many of them rivalling and sometime fighting over the best places closest to where the rivers actually meet.

The logistics of a Kumbh Mela is incredible. Rahul Mehrotra calls the town of tents a "pop-up megacity" and regards it as a case of "extreme urbanism". Mehrotra is editor of a book based on the research work of a project based at Harvard University to study the Kumbh Mela as exceptional temporary urban planning.[258] Tens of thousands of police officers and a range of government institutions collaborate to create a transient urban space and ensure the working of the makeshift structure for millions of pilgrims. Particular care has to be taken that there are no stampedes, which in the past have led to many casualties. Fortunately, no serious stampede has happened in recent decades through the ever-growing history of the Kumbh Mela. Epidemics or other

258 Mehrotra 2015: Introduction.

public health-disasters also have to be prevented as millions of pilgrims pass through. The mega-event is accompanied by thousands of journalists and photographers, including a great number of foreign nationals in their search for extraordinary images. The official website includes information in English and Hindi for pilgrims as well as tourists; it also offers the standard "tour-packages", including overnight stays, guide, and a secure place for the holy dip at one of the more prominent places. Tourists and pilgrims are offered to "meet the mystics and witness their miracles", to "experience the power of spirituality", and similar references to orientalist clichés that have entered the mainstream imagining of India.[259]

III. *Braj* – spiritual and geographical

Besides the classical places of pilgrimage in mainstream Hinduism that go back to the first millennium CE, there are a lot of sacred places that were "identified" as such much later. This is particularly true for the holy places – *i.e.* pilgrimage-sites – related to Kṛṣṇa. The 16th century proved to be a crucial epoch for the identification of places where Kṛṣṇa used to "play", according to the canonical account in the *Bhāgavata-Purāṇa*. The village where Kṛṣṇa grew up, Braj, was lost until then. The then recently founded school-traditions *puṣṭimārg* (founded by Vallabhācārya, *circa* 1479–1531) and *gauḍīya vaiṣṇava sampradāya* (founded by Caitanya, *circa* 1485–1533) were particularly active in this process of identification of the geographical places of Kṛṣṇa's plays. This development responded to the blossoming of devotional Krishnaism (*kṛṣṇabhakti*) during the epoch mentioned. Braj was "lost and found"[260], and Vallabhācārya personally came to the region to identify particularly the hill Govardhan, which Kṛṣṇa had lifted in order to provide a sheltered space for the village people, when Indra had sent a heavy storm. Govardhan immediately became an important pilgrimage-centre of the *puṣṭimārg*. Caitanya sent his two important pupils Sanātan och Rūp Goswāmī to Braj, who "saved" a great many "places of play" (*līlāsthal*) within the

---

[259] www.kumbh.gov.in/en (19.1.2019)

[260] Vaudeville 1976.

fifteen years of their stay. Caitanya himself discovered several places through divination, when he personally came to village Vṛndāvan in 1515 CE.[261] The traditional biography of Caitanya (*Caitanyacaritāmṛta*) in chapter 20 of the *madhyalīlā*-part reports an episode during the stay of Caitanya in Vṛndāvan, when he asked the people of the village where the Rādhākund pond was, where Kṛṣṇa and Rādhā used to "play" in the water (*jalakrīḍā*). Nobody knew. Hearing this, Caitanya started to search the village for hints, and he finally found a small pond, which he could positively confirm as the place of the *jalakrīḍā*, whereupon Caitanya and his followers, overwhelmed by the joy of having found the real place, started to sing and dance to the glory of Kṛṣṇa.[262]

It is said that some Kadamba trees in the region still bear fresh marks of Kṛṣṇa leaning against them with his crown (*mukuṭ*). In other words, Kṛṣṇa's "play" is somehow ongoing, and the divine Vṛndāvan, where Kṛṣṇa dances with the Gopīs (*rāslīlā*) eternally, somehow continually leaves its imprint on the mundane Vṛndāvan. Theologically speaking, the "play" never ended, and the interaction between the two Vṛndāvans – divine and mundane, eternal and historical – continues. It is ongoing, even though not always clearly visible.[263] The mundane *Braj mandal* – the region around Mathurā in Western Uttar Pradesh – is a world parallel to the eternal *Braj* that is not bound to time and place.

In our present dark age, the *kaliyuga* according to Hindu belief, mundane *Braj* with all the identified places of Kṛṣṇa's appearance, with all its temples and bathing-places along the Yamunā river, is but a shadow of the timeless *Braj*. The decline is clearly visible in Govardhan, which is no longer a hill, as it used to be in the time of Kṛṣṇa's pastimes, but almost flat as the rest of the landscape. Kṛṣṇa is present and absent at the same time during the modern pilgrimage. The pilgrim suffers with the Gopīs after Kṛṣṇa's leave to Mathura from his absence. Kṛṣṇa has left his marks in the region, he is somehow present, but *antardhāna*, *i.e.* he disappeared. Any visitor can observe how strong the emotional effect of this iden-

---

[261] Compare Vaudeville 1976; Entwistle 1987.

[262] Compare: www.radhanathswamiweekly.com/radhanath-swami-glories-sri-radha-kunda (19.1.2019)

[263] Vaudeville 1976; Entwistle 1987.

tification with the Gopīs can be. A strange mixture of intense joy and desperation sometimes visibly overwhelms pilgrims.

The popular versions of the *Bhāgavata-Purāṇa* in Braj or Modern Standard Hindi – as for example the much read *Premsāgar* ("Ocean of Love") of Lallūlāl – go much into the details of the exalted behaviour of the Gopīs after Kṛṣṇa had left them for themselves. They perform Kṛṣṇa's "plays", they recall what he did and what he said, they cry, consulate each other, become obsessed in panic, and faint. *Gopībhāv*, the sentiment of the Gopīs, is the highest form of spiritual consciousness in Krishnaism. Some groups, like the Haridāsīs, go as far as to enact this mystical transsexualism in practical terms: Haridāsī men may wear female clothes in Braj. The "gender of longing" is female.[264] The poetry that goes under the name of the Rajput princess Mīrābāī (1498–1547), who renounced her status in order to be Kṛṣṇa's beloved, may give a vivid example of this kind of emotion:

> With my tears,
> I watered the creeper of love that I planted;
> now the creeper has grown spread all over,
> and borne the fruit of bliss.
> The churner of the milk churned with great love.
> When I took out the butter, no need to drink any buttermilk.
> I came for the sake of love-devotion;
> seeing the world, I wept.[265]

Mīrābāī saw herself as married to a statue of the Giridhar Nāgar, *i.e.* Kṛṣṇa who holds the Govardhan-mountain above himself to protect the inhabitants of Vṛndāvan from storm. In another poem that forms part of the Sikh *Guru Granth Sāhib*, Mīrābāī is quite explicit on the pain she is suffering because of Kṛṣṇa's absence:

> Arrows like spears: this body is pierced
> and, Mother, he's gone far away.
> When did it happen, Mother? I don't know
> but now it's too much to bear.[266]

---

[264] Hawley 2005:167 on Mīrābāī.
[265] Mīrābāī 1980, translation by Anthony Alston.
[266] Translation by Hawley 2005:168.

The hymn is a dialog between a Gopī and her mother, pointing to the lover that abandoned her, but on a spiritual level it is about the experiences of the believer with the absent God. In 16th century Krishnaism, Kṛṣṇa's absence ranges among the most prominent subjects. Even though *viyoga* (separation) dominates over *saṃyoga* (being together), the Gopīs are continuously convinced that their emotional form of *bhakti* (devotion) is more substantial than the more abstract *advaita vedānta*. This becomes particularly clear in the dialog with Kṛṣṇa's messenger Uddhava in Braj, given in *Bhāgavata-Purāṇa* 10.48. Uddhava tries to convince the Gopīs that a more detached, non-dualist spirituality is somewhat better than the emotional and even ecstatic religious performance they practice. Uddhava, however, leaves Vṛndāvan defeated. He understands that the *saguṇa* ('qualified', *i.e.* personal) form of *bhakti*, with the person of Kṛṣṇa as its centre, is the highest form of *bhakti*. The Gopīs' performative memorization of Kṛṣṇa's "play" (*līlā*) is a form of *bhakti* more advanced than what he knew until then. God is not all-over in the sense that he is invisible and formless. He manifests himself in time and space as a *pūrṇāvatāra* ('full manifestation'). In brief, monotheism is more advanced than monism.

IV. Traditional and contemporary pilgrimage

The pilgrimage to mundane Braj plays an important role for Krishnaites from the 16th century onwards, when the canonical list of holy places was basically laid out. The sacred landscape is constantly enlarged and revised until today.[267] One of the more recent innovation for example is the "temple of the foreigners" (*aṅgrezoṃ kā mandir*), as the Sri Sri Krishna Balaram Mandir[268] (ISKCON or Hare Krishna Temple) is conveniently called in Hindi. The construction of the 1970s was not particularly welcomed in Vṛndāvan, especially after rumors about drug-trafficking and a murder-case on the temple-compound in the late 1980. Compared with the more traditional temples in the vicinity, the Hare Krishna temple cannot claim particular importance, but the presence of foreign devotees has a certain attraction,

[267] Vaudeville 1976; Entwistle 1987.

[268] www.iskconvrindavan.com (6.10.2020). The temple name in Latin script is used in all languages that are offered on the website.

particularly their dancing in the temple, which marks the place as one of the attractions of Vṛndāvan for the pilgrims, much to the chagrin of the leadership of the more traditional orders. The relationship between different sacred places is also a relationship between different school-traditions and the temples they are related to. The *status quo* provides the basic terms of reference; that is why it is difficult for new formations like the Hare Krishna to intrude into the territory, even though they are economically strong and provide foreign devotees, who contribute to the attraction of the place. The Govardhan hill, however, is basically *puṣṭimārg* territory. The famous Giridhar Nāgar in the *puṣṭimārg* temple was initially installed in the 1520s. Non-*puṣṭimārgī*s stay away from the temple-compound and very often from the mount itself. Instead, the circumambulation is a common way of pilgrimage, affirming the sacred status of the mount.

The discovery of places of Kṛṣṇa's "play" in Braj goes hand in hand with the production of narrations of the places and their relation to Kṛṣṇa, the so-called *sthalalīlā*s (local plays). Besides, lyric hymns on certain holy places (*sthalapurāṇā*s, *sthalamahātmya*s) were constantly produced and – continuously important even today – descriptions of the attractions in the forest around Vṛndāvan that the pilgrim might come across while circumambulating Vṛndāvan (*vanparikramā*). Popular pamphlets with these hymns in Braj and Sanskrit are still on sale at many places at the places visited by pilgrims. Vṛndāvan is a growing town of about 65.000 inhabitants according to the 2011 census. Unfortunately, there is not much left of the mystical groves, where Kṛṣṇa is said to have met his Gopīs overnight, that still existed in earlier centuries.

The fame of the Braj region has much to do with the missionary activities of Krishnaism and popular hymns. Particularly important are the hymns composed by a group of poets called Aṣṭachāp, eight poets that are believed to belong to the *puṣṭimārg* school, the undisputedly most famous of them being Sūrdās (1478?-1583?).[269] As in the case of almost all devotional poets in a period of South Asian history, often called Early Modernity in more recent research, the historical figure of the poet is difficult to grasp beyond

[269] Other members of the Aṣṭchāp were Paramānanddās, Nanddās, Kṛṣṇadās, Govindswāmī, Kumbhandās, Chitaswāmī, and Caturbhujdās.

the traditional narratives in hagiographical literature starting with Nābhādās' *Bhaktamāl*.[270] Whether Sūrdās actually belonged to the *puṣṭimārg* or not, it is clear that he had a close relationship to the Giridhar Nāgar temple in Govardhan. His poetry, however, was adopted in Kṛṣṇa devotionalism beyond all limits and shaped the meaning of *bhakti* to quite some extent all over North India. The performance of these hymns in public space and in private was important for spreading the sense of sacredness of Braj, shaping a religious climate in which the attraction of the pilgrimage to the sacred region of Kṛṣṇa's pastimes played an important role.

V. Traditional and modern criticism of pilgrimage

In the canonical "History of Hindi literature" (*Hindī sāhitya kā itihās*, 1942), Rāmcandra Śukla defined the period between 1375 Vikrama Saṃvat and 1700 Vikrama Saṃvat (= 1317/1318–1642/1643 CE) as *bhaktikāl*, the period of devotional literature. This term is based on the theological content of some of the literature composed during this epoch; much of devotional literature that is still performed today is related to composers of *bhaktikāl*, but the extant *corpus* does not go back to manuscripts dating to the lifetime of the ascribed composers themselves. The modern *Sūrsāgar* for example, a 20th century edition of the *corpus* ascribed to Sūrdās by the Nāgarī Pracāriṇī Sabhā, contains about 5000 hymns. The tradition is cumulative, and numerous hymns that form part of the tradition have been composed in Sūrdās' style, but not by the historical composer.

What I would like to point out here is the importance of the binary of *saguṇ* and *nirguṇ* that Rāmcandra Śukla insists upon. *Saguṇ bhakti* is a devotion to a personal God, who is present in his statues, at holy places, and appears in history through a diversity of manifestations, particularly through his *avatārs*. *Nirguṇ bhakti* is supposed to focus on God's formless and universal appearance, and particularly in one's self. *Nirguṇ bhakti* is therefore critical of temple-service, bathing-rituals, social and religious hierarchies, and pilgrimage as such. The two forms of *bhakti* often go together in one way or another. Even poems under the name of Sūrdās

270 Compare Callewaert & Snell 1994.

may contain a eulogy of God as being identical with one's self. Śukla's effort was to give both forms of *bhakti* a clear-cut identity, while including them in a conclusive history of Hindi literature and Hinduism at the same time.

One of the most prominent devotional poets of the *nirguṇ bhakti* tradition is Ravidās (15th–16th century), a contemporary of Caitanya and Vallabhācārya. As in the case of Sūrdās, it is hardly possible to decide on the original *corpus* of Ravidās; much of the poetry that is ascribed to him is not composed by the historical poet-saint. One poem ascribed to Ravidās goes like this:

> Where should I go?
> You are everywhere.[271]

And the poem continues:

> Why do you hold back your love, Keśav?
> Remove my misfortune!
> Ravidās says, I have become completely absent –
> My mind fled, where should I go?
> You are everywhere, Lord Govinda,
> I am immersed within You alone.

In other words: the suffering from Kṛṣṇa's absence is detached from any geographical space. The poem transforms the focus on Kṛṣṇa into a more monistic, panentheist interpretation of God's reality within the world. The hymn can illustrate the transformation of Krishnaism into some form of iconoclastic monism, which does not leave any room for sacredness of a geographical space. The hagiographical sources clearly report how this conceptualization of Krishnaism is related to the protest against the social hierarchy along caste lines.[272] Perhaps the most famous saying of the tanner (*camār*) Ravidās is: *man caṅgā to kaṭhorī meṃ gaṅgā*, "If the hart is pure, the Gaṅgā can be found in a small vessel (filled with water)". In other word, purification is not bound to the access to prestigious bathing-places that are reserved for caste Hindus, particularly at Banaras and other famous places of pilgrimage along the river Gaṅgā.

---

271 Ravidās 38 in Callewaert & Friedlander 1992:127.
272 Hawley 2005:64.

While the historical Kabīr, like Ravidās, was based in Banaras, perhaps the most prestigious places of pilgrimage along the Gaṅgā, many poems in the Kabīr tradition explicitly declare the pilgrimage to Kāśī (Banaras) as well as the pilgrimage to Mekka as being meaningless. Similarly, *mandir* (temple) and *masjid* (mosque) have no meaning. Instead, God dwells in the human self and nowhere else:

> There is nothing but water in the holy pools.
> I know, I have been swimming in them.
> All the gods, sculpted of wood or ivory can't say a word.
> I know, I have been crying out to them.
> The Sacred Books of the East are nothing but words.
> I looked through their covers one day sideways.
> What Kabīr talks of is only what he has lived through.
> If you have not lived through something, it is not true.[273]

VI. From performance to transformation

Another case of religious criticism of pilgrimage is to be found in the Sikh tradition, another product of South Asia's impressive transreligious spirituality of the Early Modern epoch. According to the traditional biography (*Janamsākhī*), Guru Nānak (1469–1538), the historical founder of the Sikh religion, used to travel from one holy place to another during a long period of his life. He was particularly interested in visiting traditional places of pilgrimage – Muslim and Hindu. The story of his visit to Mekka and Medina are well known in the Sikh community until today. Though being non-Muslim, he turned towards Muslims with his message that the real pilgrimage to Mekka is not a physical journey, but a spiritual.

Janamsākhī 5 reports Nānak's spectacular fourth travel towards the West, to Mekka and Medina: He started to wear shoes made from leather and even leather-pants. He put a garland of bones around his neck and painted a red point on his forehead. As a child he used to wear blue clothes and now once again he put on blue clothes when he went to Mekka. He met a Hajjī (pilgrim to

---

[273] Bly 2004:44.

Mekka) and put up a joint overnight-stay. The Hajjī asked him: "My Darvīś (holy man), you don't have a wooden beggar's bowl, no leather-bag, no marijuana-pipe – nothing! Are you Hindu or Muslim?" Nānak answered:

> The Fear of You, o Lord God, is my marijuana;
> my consciousness is the pouch which holds it.
> I have become an intoxicated hermit.
> My hands are my begging bowl;
> I am so hungry for the Blessed Vision of Your Darshan.
> I beg at Your Door, day after day.
> I long for the Blessed Vision of Your Darshan.
> I am a beggar at Your Door – please bless me with Your charity.[274]

Darśan – in *bhakti*-terminology the visible appearance, for example of the Lord in the temple in form of his statue or of sacred places – is a centrepiece of Hindu devotionalism. Nānak transforms the traditional meaning of *darśan* into something that no longer relates to a fixed location. *Darśan* is a form of spiritual presence in front of the non-worldly divine. Nānak is a radical critique of the institution of pilgrimage. At the same time, certain holy places of the Sikhs developed into places of pilgrimage in the young Sikh community, starting during Guru Nānak's lifetime.

Nānak's relation to pilgrimage as an institution was paradoxical. He used to join pilgrimage-parties disguised as a pilgrim in order to preach about how useless the belief in the religious reward for religious journeying was. One of these journeys, mentioned in the *Janamsākhī*, was a visit at the Kumbh Mela in Allahabad. Nānak's spiritual friend and pupil Mardānā, a Muslim musician, accompanied him. They used to sit in the camp of the pilgrims and attract people to them by singing and holding sermons. Some monastic orders (*akhāṛā*) that had their camps close by considered killing Nānak, since he distracted pilgrims from meeting the monks and explained to them how useless it was to go on pilgrimage. One day Nānak followed one of the abbots (*mahant*s) of an *akhāṛā* to the Gaṅgā, where the *mahant* would take his holy dip in the water; the following dialogue is reported:

---

[274] *Guru Granth Sahib* 721: www.srigurugranth.org/0721.html (24.1.2019)

> In a soft, gentle but clear voice he asked the *mahant*: 'Why did you bathe in the river?' 'Why did I bathe in the river?' the *mahant* repeated Nanak's words incredulously. 'You know well enough why we all bathed in the river. It was to wash away our sins.' 'What did you wash with your bath?' 'My body', the *mahant* replied, not yet getting the drift of Nanak's subtle questioning. 'Did your body commit your sins?'[275]

Nānak's point is that ritual purification with water is useless, since *the person* is responsible for his sin (*pāp*), not his body. Purification is an inner process that involves the mind.

The *Janamsākhīs* are full of this kind of narratives, in which Nānak does not teach directly, but demonstrates the absurdity of certain religious acts and beliefs by questioning the believers – the "maieutic" method of Socrates. In the end, many of the listeners to Nānak's questioning become aware of the wrongs of their doings or beliefs and, in the case of the abbots at the Kumbh Mela, Nānak ends up turning against his earlier conviction on the usefulness of pilgrimage and ritual purification by the Gaṅgā's water.

VII. Conclusion

Reform Hinduism of the 19th and 20th centuries overwhelmingly followed the arguments against physical pilgrimage and either radically turned against it or believed in the metaphorical form of pilgrimage as spiritual transformation. The revival of *vedānta* tried to distinguish itself from the ascription of the divine to images, temples, ritual oblation, and places of pilgrimage. Besides, colonial *vedānta* often could see nothing but the superstition of pilgrims and the exploitation-strategies of greedy traders of religion in the notorious Paṇḍās, the priests at places of pilgrimage. If they had a positive attitude to the vocabulary of pilgrimage, it would be as metaphors for spiritual transformation.

This aversion to the localization of sacredness and the whole idea of spiritual transformation is present even in Mahatma Gandhi's critical statements on Zionism. The true Zion, he writes, is spiritual and not located in the outer world.

---

[275] Dhillon 2015:116f.

> Zionism in its spiritual sense is a lofty aspiration. By spiritual sense I mean they should want to realize the Jerusalem that is within. Zionism meaning re-occupation of Palestine has no attraction to me. ... The real Zionism of which I have given you my meaning is the thing to strive for, long for and die for. Zion lies in one's heart. It is the abode of God. The real Jerusalem is the spiritual Jerusalem. Thus he can realize this Zionism in any part of the world.[276]

Even Hermann Kallenbach, Gandhi's German-Jewish friend and supporter from his early activist days in South Africa, could not win over Gandhi's support for the Zionist movement, when he was sent by the World Zionist Organisation to India. Not even the open and massive antisemitism in Nazi Germany made Gandhi warm up for the idea of a Jewish state in Palestine; he insisted on a spiritualized conception of Zion. Gandhi used a trope that goes back to *nirguṇ bhakti*, in which the pilgrimage is a description of an inner travel, rather than a physical, and a form of spiritual transformation. Kabir says in one of his most famous couplets:

> Musk is in the navel; the hare looks out for it all over the forest (without finding it).
> In this way, God is to be found in everyone; the world doesn't see him.[277]

The *saguṇ bhakti*, however, continually supported the idea of localization of the sacred and of spiritual rewards through pilgrimage. In historical practice, *saguṇ* and *nirguṇ* somehow went hand in hand. The distinctive identities of the two types of *bhakti*, which Śukla tries to establish, are somewhat artificial. They do not mark exclusive alternatives, but two ends of a spectrum with authors and traditions floating freely between the two. Beyond that, the two types of *bhakti* inspire each other mutually and craft their identity in constant interaction with each other. As for many poetical traditions, looking into the detail of the theological

---

[276] Interview in *The Jewish Chronicle*, London, October 2, 1931. Chapter 5 in Lev 2012 looks in more depth into the complex relationship of Gandhi to the idea of Zionism and Judaism. Thanks to Shimon Lev for this reference.

[277] *kastūrī kuṇḍal basai mrigā ḍhūṃḍhai ban māhīṃ / aise ghaṭ ghaṭ meṃ rām hai duniyā dekhai nāhīṃ //* (Kabīr 1957:76)

content, *sagun̩* and *nirgun̩* hardly form excluding alternatives, but rather mark the poles within the open range of devotional options.

It can be difficult to decide in detail whether a certain poem is more towards one pole of meaning or the other, *sagun̩* or *nirgun̩*. One of the efforts which negotiates between personalism and monism is the doctrine of the divine as being *acintya bhedābheda*, unthinkable separate and non-separate (from the individual self) at the same time. This theological argument is taken up by ISKCON-founder Prabhupad in the paradoxical formula (in English) "Supreme Personality of Godhead", which is the subtitle of his book about Kṛṣṇa[278], a formula that can only be understood in the context of the Indian tradition of reasoning on the nature of the divine and its manifestations, on the non-personal divine and the divine as person. The theological discourse on pilgrimage in Hindu tradition as a whole is embedded into the context of this discourse. The question is: How and where exactly does God manifest himself?

References

Ali, Daud. 2000. "From Nayika to Bhakta: A Genealogy of Female Subjectivity in Early Medieval India". In: Leslie, J. & McGee, M. (eds.), *Invented Identities: The Interplay of Gender, Religion, and Politics in India*, Delhi: Oxford University Press.

Bakker, H. T. (ed.). 1990. *The History of Sacred Places in India as Reflected in Traditional Literature*. Leiden: Brill.

Berreman, Gerald D. 1963. *Hindus of the Himalayas*. Berkeley: University of California Press.

Bharati, Agehananda. 1963. "Pilgrimage in the Indian tradition." In: *History of Religion* 3, 135–167.

Bhardwaj, Surinder Mohan. 1973. *Hindu Places of Pilgrimage in India: A Study in Cultural Geography*. Berkeley: University of California Press.

——— 1985. "Religion and circulation: Hindu pilgrimage". In: Prothero, R. M. & Chapman, M. (eds.), *Circulation in Third World Countries*. London: Routledge, 241–261.

[278] www.krsnabook.com (19.1.2019)

Bly, Robert. 2004. *Kabir: Ecstatic Poems*. Boston: Beacon Press.

Bremer, Thomas S. 2005. "Tourism and religion". In: *Encyclopedia of Religion* (ed. Jones, 2nd ed.) 13, Detroit, MI: Macmillan Reference USA, 9260–9264.

Callewaert, Winand M. & Friedlander, Peter G. 1992. *The life and works of Raidās*. New Delhi: Manohar.

Callewaert, Winand M. & Snell, Rupert (ed.). 1994. *According to Tradition: Hagiographical Writing in India*. Wiesbaden: Otto Harrassowitz.

Datar, Balwant N. 1961. *Himalayan Pilgrimage*. Delhi: Publication Division, Government of India.

Dhillon, Harish. 2015. *Janamsakhis: Ageless stories, Timeless Values*. New Delhi: Hay House.

Eck, Diana. 1981. "India's Tirthas: 'Crossing' in Sacred Geography". In: *History of Religions* 21, 323–344.

Entwistle, Alan W. 1987. *Braj: Centre of Krishna Pilgrimage*. Groningen: Egbert Forsten.

Feldhaus, Anne. 2003. *Connected Places: Religion, Pilgrimage, and Geographical Imagination in India*. New York: Palgrave Macmillan.

Glasenapp, Helmuth von. 1928. *Heilige Stätten Indiens*. München: Georg Müller Verlag.

Hawley, John Stratton. 2005. *Three Bhakti Voices: Mirabai, Surdas, and Kabir in Their Times and Ours*. New Delhi: Oxford University Press.

Jacobsen, Knut A. 2009. "Tīrtha and tīrthayātrā: salvific space and pilgrimage". In: *Brill's Encyclopedia of Hinduism* (ed. Jacobsen), Leiden: Brill, 381–410.

Kabīr: Vaudeville, Ch. 1957. *Kabir Granthavali (Doha). Avec introduction, traduction et notes*. Pondichéry: Institut Français d'Indologie (Publications de l'Institut Français d'Indologie 12.

Lev, Shimon. 2012. *Soulmates: The Story of Mahatma Gandhi and Hermann Kallenbach*. Delhi: Orient BlackSwan.

Lochtefeld, James. 2010. *God's Gateway: Identity and Meaning in a Hindu Pilgrimage Place*. New Delhi: Oxford University Press.

Mehrotra, Rahul (ed.). 2015. *Kumbh Mela: Studying the Ephemeral Megacity*. Ostfildern: Hatje Cantz.

Mīrābāī: Alston, A. J. 1980. *The Devotional Poems of Mirabai: Translated*. New Delhi: Motilal Banarsidass.

Saha, Shandip. *Creating a Community of Grace: A History of the Pusti Marga in Northern and Western India*. www.columbia.edu /cgi-bin/cul/resolve?AQP0595 (17.1.2019)

Singh, Rana P.B. 2006. "Pilgrimage in Hinduism: Historical Context and Modern Perspectives". In: Timothy, Dallen J. & Olsen, Daniel H. (eds.), *Tourism, Religion, and Spiritual Journeys*. London: Routledge, 220–236.

Stausberg, Michael. 2010. *Religion und moderner Tourismus*. Berlin: Verlag der Weltreligionen.

Śukla, Rāmcandra. 1942. *Hindī sāhitya kā itihās*. Vārāṇasī: Nāgarī Pracāriṇī Sabhā. [Many reprints].

Vaudeville, Charlotte. 1976. "Braj, Lost and Found". In: *Indo-Iranian Journal* 18, 195–213.

——— 1993. *A Weaver Named Kabir*. Delhi: Oxford University Press.

6. Buddhist Surrealists in Bengal

Per Kværne

Abstract

Towards the end of the first millennium CE, Buddhism in Bengal was dominated by the Tantric movement, characterized by an external/physical as well as internal/meditational *yoga*, believed to lead to spiritual enlightenment and liberation from the round of birth and death. This technique and its underlying philosophy were expressed in the *Caryāgīti*, a collection of short songs in Old Bengali composed by a category of poets and practitioners of *yoga*, some of whom apparently had a peripatetic lifestyle. One of the peculiarities of Old Bengali is the presence of a large number of homonyms, permitting play on ambiguous images. This, it is argued in the first part of the chapter, is the key to understanding many songs that are seemingly meaningless or nonsensical, or that could be superficially taken to be simply descriptions of everyday life in the countryside of Bengal. By means of their very form, the songs convey the idea of the identity of the secular and the spiritual, of time and eternity. The second part of the chapter makes a leap in time, space, and culture, by suggesting a resonance for the *Caryāgīti* in the Surrealist Movement of Western art.

I

Having milked the tortoise
the basket cannot hold –

How to cite this book chapter:
Kværne, P. 2021. Buddhist Surrealists in Bengal. In: Larsson, S. and af Edholm, K. (eds.) *Songs on the Road: Wandering Religious Poets in India, Tibet, and Japan*. Pp. 113–126. Stockholm: Stockholm University Press. DOI: https://doi.org/10.16993/bbi.f.

the alligator devours the tamarind of the tree.
The courtyard is in the house –
listen, o dancing-girl!
The rag was carried off by the thief at midnight.

The mother-in-law fell asleep,
the daughter-in-law stays awake.
The rag was carried off by the thief –
where shall one go to search for it?
By day the crow frightens the daughter-in-law –
by night she goes to meet her lover.
The noble Kukkuri sings of such conduct –
among millions, it has entered but a single heart.[279]

This enigmatic song is one of the approximately fifty short poems that constitute a collection known as the *Caryāgīti*, 'Songs of (Yogic) Practice'. This collection of poems is generally regarded as one of the very last Buddhist texts to have been composed and committed to writing in India, perhaps in the 12th century. They are written in a language usually referred to as Old Bengali, and constitute the earliest literary work preserved in any modern Indo-Aryan language, or, put more simply, in any major language in North India.[280]

It is not so easy to understand what the poet, Kukkuri, is trying to say, so let us start by reading one more song, before we attempt to understand them.

The boat of Compassion is filled with gold –
silver has been left on the shore.
Steer on, o Kamali, towards the sky!
Birth is no more – how can it come back?
The peg is pulled up, the rope cast off –
ask your Guru, o Kamali, and steer on!

Ascending the stern, he gazes in all directions.
There is no oar –
how can you row across the river?

---

[279] Kværne 1986 (1977). The song quoted is number 2 according to the standard sequence of the songs.

[280] Kværne 1986 (1977).

Ascending the stern,
he presses the oar to the right and the left –
thus he finds great happiness on the way.[281]

We are in Bengal, the land of languid rivers, where boats have always been the most important means of transport. But how does this glimpse of timeless daily life disclose a spiritual dimension? Is there a secret message hidden behind the image?

We might begin by noting that most of the poems in the *Caryāgīti* use images from nature and from rural life in Bengal. Were the authors of the songs "wandering poets"? Certainly, some of them were itinerant, especially Kaṇha (or Kṛṣṇa), the most prolific of the poets, to whom no less than twelve songs are attributed. He calls himself a *kāpālika*, a homeless *yogin* who frequents the charnel-grounds and drinks from a human skull (Sanskrit *kapāla*). Kaṇha's songs describe the life of such *yogin*s, as well as their female partners, *yoginī*s. Together they challenge the conventions of society and roam about naked, their bodies smeared with ashes from fires where corpses are cremated. They wear ornaments carved from human bones and use sexual techniques to achieve spiritual enlightenment – or at least, so it is claimed in the songs.

However, a number of the poets may be regarded as "wanderers" in a wider sense, for while some – potters and weavers – live in villages, the way of life of others – hunters and arrow-makers – define them as "outsiders". In an existential sense, at least, they are wanderers, being despised and rejected. Gundari was a hunter of birds. Śabara belonged to the jungle-dwelling tribe of Sabar or Saora, which still lives in the forests of Central India and West Bengal.[282] Bhade was a painter, Tantri a weaver, Saraha an arrow-maker, and Kaṇha was, as mentioned, an itinerant *yogin*. All of these poet-*yogin*s, however, whether villagers or itinerant, crowd together on the lowest rungs of the social ladder, on the very margins of society, in the company of prostitutes and *yoginī*s. They live on the periphery of society, in a kind of social no-man's land.

[281] Kværne 1986 (1977), song 8. The boat is propelled by stern sculling.
[282] Cf. Mahaswati Devi 2002.

This is the kind of individuals that in the songs declare themselves to be their authors, each song normally ending with a line where the author discloses his name. In this way, the songs are attributed to a particular category of *yogins*, known from other sources and belonging to the late Buddhist tradition of India. They are usually called *siddha*, a Sanskrit word literally meaning 'accomplished', but which might be translated in this context as 'spiritual master', one whose accomplishment is to have obtained release from the round of birth and death in the wheel of transmigration.

It is worth noting that the poetic and religious tradition of the *siddhas* continued to exert an influence even after Buddhism practically disappeared from Bengal at the same time as the Muslim conquest in the 13th century. Thus, the erotic terminology in the *caryā*-songs has probably left an imprint on the later Hindu poetry in Bengal with its emphasis on the love between the deity in the form of Kṛṣṇa and the soul, envisaged as Rādhā, Kṛṣṇa's passionately enamoured mistress.[283] The most important and direct heritage of the *Caryāgīti*, however, is beyond doubt to be found in the songs of the Bauls of Bengal, itinerant devotees of "the Divine Spark" manifesting itself in the hidden depths of the soul, a divinity they worship through songs full of longing and passion and images reminiscent of those found in the *Caryāgīti*. The Bauls, still a living tradition, in turn inspired Rabindranath Tagore, and through him, modern Bengali culture and literature as a whole.[284] For this reason there is still a considerable interest in the *Caryāgīti* in literary and academic circles in West Bengal as well as in Bangla Desh.

Ever since the songs were published for the first time in 1916,[285] it has been generally taken for granted that the concrete, everyday images they contain in such abundance have an immediately understandable significance as well as a deeper, hidden meaning. That this is the case, is evident not only from the very form of many of the songs, where philosophical concepts are linked with objects from daily life such as "the boat of compassion", and so on, but more particularly by the fact that the songs, in the manuscript

283 Dimock 1989.

284 Openshaw 2002.

285 Shastri (ed.) 2006.

in which they have been preserved, are inserted in a learned commentary where each song is interpreted and commented on.

This commentarial text is a late example of the Buddhist scholarly tradition in India – it is composed in Sanskrit, the language of learning, and abounds in quotations from other Sanskrit texts. Composed by an otherwise unknown scholar by the name of Munidatta, it is based on a unified, coherent interpretation of the songs in terms of a yogic system. According to Munidatta, therefore, the concrete images are to be understood as allusions to the body's energy-centres, the so-called *cakra*s, 'wheels', that are activated by means of specific meditational and physiological techniques. Among these techniques are breath-control and certain ways of manipulating sexual energy, represented by the male sexual fluid. By means of these techniques the *siddha* obtains a state of boundless bliss, in which all concepts of contrast or duality, such as "subject" and "object", "then" and "now", "I" and "other" are transcended and eliminated.

Previous translators and interpreters have generally read the songs in terms of Munidatta's commentary. I, too, used the commentary in my doctoral dissertation, published in 1977.[286] I shall return to my interpretation below. At the same time, the majority of those who have published translations of the songs have been fascinated by the concrete images, and understood them as realistic and factual descriptions of the nature and culture of Bengal a thousand years ago. As an example of the emphasis placed on these concrete images, I shall quote from a study of the songs by Hasna Jasinuddin Moudud, a prominent figure on the cultural scene in Bangla Desh, published in 1992.[287] She writes perceptively as follows about the imagery of the songs:

> They give us a vivid account of the life and occupations of the common people, their work, events of birth, marriage and death, religious activities, dress and ornaments, food and utensils, and music and musical instruments. There is also a beautiful description of the riverine and green eastern part of

[286] Kværne 1977. See first note.

[287] Moudud 1992. For Moudud's translation, see also: http://vajrayana.faithweb.com/rich_text_3.html

> Bengal which is Bangla Desh today. The poems describe rivers, canals, ponds, muddy shores, various types of boats and their different parts, ferrying and rowing; all these were used... as spiritual symbols.[288]

She also writes:

> From the Caryas one can get a vivid account of the life and professions of the common people. Rice was the staple food. Bulls were used for cultivation and cows were kept for milk. Wine making and drinking was common to men and women. Playing chess is mentioned in the Caryas. The use of gold and silver were common. Dancing and singing were considered natural activities. Hunting, weaving and ferrying represented different occupations.[289]

One naturally wonders whether there is a set pattern or system according to which images inspired by the mundane, visible world would consistently point to *yoga*-techniques and states of meditation related to the path of the *siddha*s towards ultimate enlightenment and release from birth and death. Scholars who have discussed this question have taken such corresponding meanings for granted, and with regard to certain key images this is no doubt true. Thus, the image of the *yoginī* certainly represents the absolute freedom of spiritual enlightenment, for the central psychic energy-channel which follows the *yogin*'s spine leads to the *cakra* of concentrated psychic power, located at the top of the head, the *locus* of the experience of absolute, liberating bliss. However, the central psychic channel can also be represented, according to Munidatta, by various women, all mentioned in the songs: a woman of the *śabara*-people, living in the jungle; or a *ḍombī*, a woman of the despised outcaste *ḍom*-people; or the spouse of the unclean and casteless *caṇḍāla*, whose task it was (and still is) to handle the cremation of corpses, the most potent source of ritual pollution; or a *śundinī*, the young woman who produces and serves alcohol, another despised and unclean activity. All these women come from the margins of society, yet all can represent the state of ultimate release from birth and death.

---

288 Moudud 1992:1.

289 Moudud 1992:41.

However, the message of the songs – and of Munidatta's commentary – is more complex than these images might suggest. There is a duality, an absolute contrast of meaning, in many of the images. One and the same image can represent concepts pointing to release *as well as* pointing to the state of bondage in the material world of birth and death. The interpretation offered by Munidatta in his commentary of one and the same image sometimes points in one direction, sometimes in the opposite direction. For example, the image of the *tree* can symbolize the state of absolute freedom, but also the physical body. The *river* can indicate the central psychic energy-channel along the spine, but the entire system of psychic veins and arteries can also be an image of the illusory nature of existence in the world. The *ocean* can be the infinite luminosity of ultimate bliss in which all things and all concepts dissolve, but also the enslaving round of birth and death. In the same way, one could continue adding example to example.[290]

It would be overhasty to draw the conclusion that the message of the *siddha*s as expressed in the songs is reproduced in the learned Sanskrit commentary of Munidatta, in which everything is interpreted according to a specific system of *yoga*. To me it is clear that there is an *inherent* ambiguity in many of the images found in the *Caryāgīti*. This ambiguity, I argue, is in many cases due to the fact that the phonetic development of different Sanskrit words results in a single phonetic form in the *Caryāgīti*;[291] in other words, what we find are *homonymous* words. This is by no means unusual in the early forms of North Indian languages, such as Hindi or Bengali, that have their origin in Sanskrit.

Just to give a couple of examples, I could cite the word *kāu* in the first song quoted, derived from Sanskrit *kāka*, 'crow'. However, it could just as well be derived from Sanskrit *kāya*, 'body', which is what Munidatta assumes. In the second song quoted, *rūpā* comes from Sanskrit *rūpya*, 'silver', but could also, as Munidatta suggests, be understood as derived from *rūpa*, 'form', in the sense of 'tangible form'. In the same song, *sone* could be derived from

[290] For a detailed survey of these images, see Kværne 1977:*passim*.

[291] Kværne 1977:54–55.

suvarṇa, 'gold', but just as well from *śūnya*, 'emptiness'. So while I have translated literally: "The boat of Compassion is filled with gold – silver has been left on the shore", Munidatta's commentary would give an interpretation as follows: "The enlightened mind was filled by the absence of concepts – the material world was left behind".[292] Many similar examples could be cited.

Besides homonymy, Munidatta makes use of artificial etymologies when interpreting words in the *Caryāgīti*. In this way he can ascribe to a word a profound or esoteric meaning for which there is no linguistic justification. Having said that, however, it should be added that some of these artificial etymologies were probably widely accepted in learned Buddhist and Hindu circles at the time of Munidatta, that is the 12th or 13th centuries, and may well have corresponded to the understanding of the *siddha*s themselves. To take but one example, the word *duli* in the first song means 'tortoise'. This word is interpreted – in a totally artificial way – by splitting it into two components: *du* and *li*. *Du* is, so Munidatta claims, derived from Sanskrit *dvaya*, 'two', understood as 'duality' (Munidatta: *dvaya-ākāram*), while *li*, he maintains, is the verbal stem *lī*, 'to be dissolved, disappear'. Hence Munidatta interprets *duli* as the psychic energy-centre at the top of the head, the *locus* where 'duality is dissolved', also referred to as 'the lotus of great bliss' – not quite the same as a 'tortoise'.

The kind of paradoxical, even nonsensical imagery found in the *caryā*-songs is routinely called *sandhyābhāṣā* in the commentary of Munidatta, and this term is found in other, similar late Indian Buddhist texts as well. However, while the term is often translated 'twilight-language', there is no consensus as to how it should be understood.[293] Those who prefer the idea of 'twilight-language' have argued, to quote just one opinion, that "Sandhyābhāṣā is a language of light and darkness; some passage can be understood, others cannot".[294] Other translations are 'intentional speech', an interpretation which has been accepted by several scholars but which is flawed by the fact that it presupposes an emendation which is not attested in any of the manuscripts. 'Enigmatic speech'

[292] Kværne 1977:104.
[293] Kværne 1977:37.
[294] Shastri 1916.

was proposed as early as 1852 by the great French Orientalist Eugène Burnouf, accepted by Shashibhushan Dasgupta in 1946,[295] and taken up again by the late David Snellgrove.[296] These translations have one thing in common, namely that they assume that the *siddha*s did not wish to impart their teachings in direct, unambiguous terms. There are, however, a couple of further explanations as well, for example that the purpose was to provide "catch-phrases to the common people", or even that "twilight-language" – the term I personally favour – was meant to be a joke.[297]

I shall not give any more examples, but proceed to my conclusion, which is my contribution to the interpretation of these songs, namely: in many of them, though not necessarily in all, it is the phonetic, formal aspect of the language of the poems – in other words, a language which is on the threshold between a late, Sanskrit-derived Middle Indian language and a modern North Indian language – which expresses, through its frequent use of homonyms and artificial etymologies, the concurrence and perfect coincidence of the relative and the absolute, the visible, material world and the invisible liberation from birth and death. It is this concurrence that is the very basis of the doctrine and practice of the *siddha*s. It is for this reason that the *siddha*s were generally strangers to the Buddhist monastic tradition. In fact, they made a point of placing themselves outside the norms and conventions of society at large, through their lifestyle as well as their philosophy. It is a paradox that it did not take long before their songs became, as we have seen, the subject of a learned commentary, and later on they were incorporated in the Tibetan collection of sacred scriptures, the doctrinal backbone of monastic, institutionalized Buddhism in Tibet.

II

It would be tempting – and certainly useful – to give a more coherent presentation of the religious system underlying the songs according to Munidatta's commentary. However, I will attempt a

[295] Dasgupta 1946.
[296] Snellgrove 1987:161f.
[297] Agehananda Bharati, quoted in Kværne 1977:38.

different approach. Keeping the ambiguity of the linguistic form of the songs in mind, I will make a leap through time and space, and without any pretence of historical or cultural continuity, land at an entirely different cultural phenomenon. I shall consider – irresponsibly, perhaps – that a certain degree of common ground in terms of basic perception of the nature of existence may be discerned in two widely separated historical and cultural contexts.

In the early 1920s, a movement appeared in Western Europe that became known as *Surrealism*. This movement was, in historical terms, a child of the Modernism that came to dominate the art scene early in the 20th century, especially Cubism, represented by painters in Paris such as Pablo Picasso and Georges Braque, as well as the Italian Futurists, represented by members of the Italian *avant-garde* such as Giacomo Balla and Umberto Boccioni. Both these movements were characterized by their focus on *dissolving the tangible form of objects*: Cubism by dissolving objects and then re-assembling them in new and surprising ways, Futurism by exploring ways of depicting speed and dynamic motion by avoiding to give objects stability and solidity on the canvas. Taking this as a point of departure, the Surrealists took one more step ahead, not by dissolving form as such, but by *completely dissolving the conventional meaning of objects*, creating instead a world based on the "logic" of dreams and the sub-conscious, a world where there is neither up nor down, where the distinction between animals and humans is blurred, where what counts is the ambivalent, paradoxical, contradictory.

In this it is not difficult to see (or so I would maintain) a parallel, at least in imagery, to the *caryā*-songs. As the great spokesman of the Surrealists, André Breton, said: "What is admirable about the fantastic is that there is no longer anything fantastic: there is only the real".[298] The *siddha*s could not have put it more pointedly: it is that which is paradoxical that is "real", and reality itself is expressed by them in what they called 'the twilight-language' (*sandhyābhāṣā*), the speech of ambivalence, of twilight, midway between light and darkness, which points to "reality" precisely through its ambiguity. I would like to illustrate this approach to

[298] Spies & Rewald (eds.) 2005:89.

reality by looking at some of the paintings of the Surrealist painter Max Ernst (1891–1976).[299] In the painting "Oedipus Rex" (1922), one observes three fingers of a hand emerging from a window to the left, holding a walnut and what appears to be a bow, while the nut is pierced by an arrow. To the right are two heads, one of a bird and another of a less easily identified creature. In the distant sky floats a tiny balloon. However, the proportion between the window and the hand is completely unbalanced. It is by no means clear what meaning, if any, the painting communicates. Still, it is difficult to avoid the impression that it *does* have a meaning, but if so, that meaning is precisely 'surrealistic' and cannot be uncovered by applying rational or empirical criteria. In fact, it is not certain that the meaning can be formulated in definable concepts or ideas at all.

Double meaning is often a basic theme in the art of Max Ernst, just as we have seen is the case in the *caryā*-songs. In the painting "Castor et Pollution" (1923), two nearly identical male heads, staring intently in opposite directions, their shoulders turned back to back, emerge from a metal container on which the words "Castor et Pollution" are written. The container seems to be placed in sea with a distant bright blue, mountainous coast in the background and spanned by a yellow sky. Ernst offers an ironical play of words with reference to the mythological twins of Antiquity, Castor and Pollux, the patron divinities of seamen. Here the parallel to the *Caryāgīti* goes further, for the twins of Antiquity have – obviously – the same mother, but – paradoxically – different fathers: the father of Castor was Tyndareus, king of Sparta, while Pollux was the divine son of Zeus himself, who in the form of a swan seduced Leda. The human and the divine constitute a pair of twins, just as the limited and the unlimited are two sides of the same coin in the world of the *caryā*-songs.

In "Birds, Fish-Snake; Scarecrow" (1921) we once again see duality represented by an enigmatic single figure with two bird's heads, placed in an inchoate and seemingly meaningless world of dreams in which various objects – a jacket, a headless woman in a pink dress, a bag with a hand emerging and touching a snake,

[299] See Spies & Rewald (eds.) 2005.

a cow that seems to be jumping over a fence, its head hidden by an outstretched hand – float about against a uniformly grey background. It is a topsy-turvy dream world of this kind that we find in one of the songs of the *Caryāgīti*:

> My house is on the hill, no neighbour have I –
> no rice in the pot, yet guests continually come!
> The frog chases the serpent –
> can milk return to the udder?
> The ox has given birth to a calf, but the cow is barren –
> the basket is milked three times a day.
>
> He who is wise, the very same is a fool –
> he who a thief, the very same is a watchman.
> Ever and ever the jackal fights with the lion –
> few are they who understand the song of the poet Dhendana![300]

One of Max Ernst's most famous (or, at the time, infamous) paintings is entitled "The Holy Virgin Chastises the Infant Jesus in the Presence of Three Witnesses: André Breton, Paul Élouard and the Artist" (1926). The Virgin Mary, complete with halo, is shown giving the child Jesus, lying face downwards on her lap, a spanking, while the heads of three representatives of the French *avant-garde* are seen watching impassively through a small opening in the wall behind Mary. That the picture created a scandal when it was first exhibited is not surprising, and Max Ernst certainly wanted to provoke conventional standards of propriety. In the same way it is not difficult to understand that in the family-centred Bengali society the *siddha* Kaṇha launched a provocation when he sings that,

> Having killed his mother-in-law,
> his aunt and sister-in-law –
> having killed his mother
> he has become an ascetic
> who drinks wine from a skull![301]

[300] Kværne 1986 (1977), song 33.
[301] Kværne 1986 (1977), song 11.

Not surprisingly, in his commentary Munidatta offers a symbolic interpretation of this verse.

An equally confusing juxtaposition of 'reality' and 'illusion' is characteristic of the art of the Belgian Surrealist René Magritte (1898–1967).[302] In his painting "The Key to the Fields" (1936), we see a window on which a landscape has been painted; however, the window is broken and has visible cracks, and what appears behind is exactly the same landscape that was painted on the window. I suggest that what Magritte wanted to do, was to challenge the traditional attempt of Western art to reproduce nature, but I would also suggest that since we are trying to "make sense of" Surrealism in terms of the *Caryāgīti*, we could view the focus of the *caryā*-songs on the identity between enlightenment and the world of birth and death as a parallel to Magritte's painting in which the coincidence of the painted window and the world outside turn out to be identical with the painting itself, the difference between them being an illusion.

Finally, in Magritte's painting "Portrait of Edward James" (1937), the English poet is standing with the back to us, facing a mirror in which, accordingly, we would expect to see his face. What we actually see, however, contradicts all logic and experience: we see an exact copy of the figure *in front of* the mirror. In other words, we are confronted by two realities: the everyday reality of a man with his back turned towards us *and* an intangible and paradoxical reality in the mirror, namely exactly the same figure with its back turned to us, not the reflexion that optical laws would lead us to expect. We are confronted with a portrait in which there is no face, which is in itself a paradox, but beyond that, we are confronted with two realities perceived at the same time, as in the *Caryāgīti*.

I am aware that my presentation of the *caryā*-songs in the light of Surrealism may be somewhat on the periphery of conventional academic norms, just as Dhendana's hut is outside the village. However, I wanted to avoid looking at these songs essentially in terms of their historical context – what came before and what came after – and running the risk of being caught in a *regressus*

302 On Magritte, see Levy 2015.

ad infinitum, a winding up of an endless historical thread. Instead I have attempted to make a leap in time and space and culture, in the hope of finding a resonance for the songs in a phenomenon in the modern world and thereby testing a new, but certainly not definitive, point of departure for understanding the enigmatic *Caryāgīti*, the Songs of (Yogic) Practice.

References

Dasgupta, Sh. 1969 (1946). *Obscure Religious Cults: As a Background of Bengali Literature*. Calcutta: K. L. Mukhopadhyay.

Dimock, Edward C. 1989. *The Place of the Hidden Moon: Erotic Mysticism in the Vaisnava-Sahajiya Cult of Bengal*. Chicago: The University of Chicago Press.

Kværne, Per. 1977. *An Anthology of Buddhist Tantric Songs: A Study of the Caryāgīti*. Oslo: Universitetsforlaget. (2nd edition, *Songs of the Mystic Path* 1986, Bangkok: White Orchid Press; 3rd edition 2010, Bangkok: Orchid Press.)

Levy, Silvano. 2015. *Decoding Magritte*. Bristol: Sansom & Co.

Mahaswati Devi. 2002. *The Book of the Hunter*. Kolkata: Seagull Books.

Moudud, Hasna Jasimuddin. 1992. *A Thousand Year Old Bengali Mystic Poetry*, Dhaka: University Press.

Openshaw, Jeanne. 2002. *Seeking Bauls of Bengal*. Cambridge: Cambridge University Press.

Shastri, Haraprasad (ed.). 2006. *Hajar Bacharer Purano Bangala Bhasay Bauddhagan o Doha* (in Bengali). Kolkata: Bangiya Sahitya Parishad.

Snellgrove, David. 1987. *Indo-Tibetan Buddhism and their Tibetan Successors*. Bangkok: Orchid Press.

Spies, Werner & Rewald, Sabine (eds.). 2005. *Max Ernst: A Retrospective*. New York: Metropolitan Museum of Art.

7. The Travels and Poems of Matsuo Bashô

Lars Vargö

Abstract

This chapter looks at the iconic 17th century Japanese poet Matsuo Bashô, who is known as the originator of *haiku* and is most famous for his travel-account *Oku no hosomichi*, 'The Narrow Road to the Interior'. This account contains many references to Buddhist temples and legends, since the purpose of the trip was not only to "be one with nature" and write poetry, but also to visit religious sites. Bashô was a Buddhist, as well as a Shintôist, a Confucian, and a Daoist. He had studied Zen Buddhism, but had enough worldly attachment to not want to enter a monastery permanently. Through his travel journals, Bashô created an ideal world of itinerant monks and he is often hailed as a role-model for wandering religious poets.

I

An important part of Japanese poetry has always been *renga* (連歌), linked poetry written by more than one poet. Already in the 12th century it was a well-developed and regulated form of literary expression. Initially, two poets would write a poem which combined one stanza consisting of 5-7-5 phonetic characters with another consisting of 7-7 characters.[303] Later it became popular

[303] Modern Japanese has two phonetic alphabets, *hiragana* and *katakana*, with 46 characters each, while older Japanese had 48 characters. With the

How to cite this book chapter:
Vargö, L. 2021. The Travels and Poems of Matsuo Bashô. In: Larsson, S. and af Edholm, K. (eds.) *Songs on the Road: Wandering Religious Poets in India, Tibet, and Japan*. Pp. 127–140. Stockholm: Stockholm University Press. DOI: https://doi.org/10.16993/bbi.g.

for several poets to create almost endless combinations of stanzas of 5-7-5 and 7-7 sound-characters.

Rules for how the stanzas should be linked became more and more complicated. The first stanza, the *hokku* (発句), set the tone for the whole poem and introduced the season by which the poem would start. The rules specified when other seasons would come in, and also when stanzas containing references to the moon, flowers, birds, love, *et cetera*, would be introduced. The poem should always look forward and, although one stanza is always associated with the previous stanza, it should not have anything to do with the one before that. It was important not to look back more than one stanza, with the exception of the last one, the *ageku* (挙句), which tied the poem together by referring to, or associating with, the theme in the *hokku*. Usually, the poet who wrote the *hokku* was the main guest of a poetry-session, and the one writing the second stanza, the *wakiku* (脇句), was the host. Therefore, the *hokku* was also a kind of greeting and often referred to something that was connected to the host, for instance the plants in his[304] garden, the view, the history of the location, specific traditions or events, *et cetera*.

In the 16th century some poets found the rules stifling and created *haikai-no-renga*, 'comic/wild/rambunctious *renga*'. A poet named Matsunaga Teitoku (松永貞徳, 1571–1654) contributed greatly to the popularization of *haikai-no-renga*. He created a special school in *haikai*-poetry, the Teimon school. Another important *haikai*-poet was Nishiyama Sôin (西山宗因, 1605–1682), who thought

exception of the five vowels and one singular consonant (the final *n*), all characters are pronounced by combining one consonant and one vowel. Thus, in poetry the characters are often referred to as *onji*, 'sound characters', or *jion*, 'character sounds'. While a syllable can contain several letters and a Japanese phonetic character has two letters in Romanization, it is written with only one written character. For instance, the name of the Swedish capital, *Stockholm*, consists of two closed syllables in Swedish or English, *Stock* and *holm*. In Japanese it is written ストックホルム, *su-to-k-ku-ho-ru-mu*, containing seven phonetic characters. The grammatical structures of Japanese and Chinese are very different from each other; in the earliest forms of written Japanese, Chinese characters were also used as phonetic characters, which were mixed with other Chinese characters used for their meaning only, making texts extremely difficult to read. Today, Chinese characters and phonetic characters are still used in combination.

[304] The poets were almost always men.

that the Teimon school had got caught in stifling rules and was too concerned with what was right and wrong. Nishiyama argued for more freedom and introduced techniques like *honkadori* (本歌取り), associations to already well-known classical poems. He and his followers formed the Danrin school.

Then came Matsuo Bashô (松尾芭蕉, 1644–1694), Japan's most well-known poet, often referred to as the originator of *haiku*. His poetry was the source of yet another school within the *haikai* tradition, the Shôfû. Bashô was not a stranger to the use of humour in his poetry, but he also stressed the need to stay away from what was too vulgar and instead underlined the necessity of creating refined and elegant poetry. He also limited the number of stanzas to 36, a format he called *kasen* (歌仙), an abbreviation for *sanjûrokkasen* (三十六歌仙), 'the 36 hermit-poets', which was a term introduced by the court-bureaucrat and poet Fujiwara no Kintô (藤原公任, 966–1041) for the most outstanding poets of his time. Bashô became a *hokku*-master and famous already in his lifetime.[305] He was constantly invited to poetry-sessions and had followers all over the country. However, Bashô was also a skillful writer of prose and his *kikô* (紀行), travel journals, and *haibun* (俳文), essays mixed with poetry, are as appreciated as his *hokku*. Bashô sometimes tired of the secular world and went on long journeys by foot and on horseback to find inspiration, pray at temples, and visit famous places. The wandering in itself served as a kind of cleansing of his spirit and he seemed to yearn for religious experiences, walking through the country as a pilgrim.

Bashô was born not far away from Kyôto, in a village called Ueno, in the ancient province of Iga, today's Mie prefecture. His family was not poor, but not particularly well-off either. His father had samurai status, but of lower rank, which forced him to also work as a farmer. As a samurai he had the privilege of having a surname. Not much is known about his mother, but on a few occasions he fondly wrote poems about her. He had one brother and four sisters. When Bashô was eighteen he began to work as

---

[305] His *hokku* is often called *haiku* and the only difference is that while a *hokku* was always followed by other stanzas, the *haiku* stands alone. The term *haiku* was coined by the poet Masaoka Shiki (正岡子規, 1867–1902), who argued that a *haiku* should free itself from linked poetry and be a poetic category of its own.

an assistant to Tôdô Yoshitada (東堂良忠, 1642–1666), an aristocrat and relative to the local lord. Yoshitada was only two years older than Bashô and they became close friends. Together they developed a strong interest in *haikai*-poetry. After only a few years together, Yoshitada suddenly died in 1666. His younger brother took his position as head of the clan and even married Yoshitada's widow. For Bashô this was a great shock and he decided that it was better to leave his village than serving someone whom he did not respect as much. To leave his village meant that he also left the expectations his family had for him and he had to give up his samurai status. There are speculations about Bashô himself having had an affair with Yoshitada's wife and that that was the real reason for his departure; true or not, Bashô would later return several times to his village for short periods.

It is not clear where Bashô immediately went after leaving Ueno, but he probably chose Kyôto, where he later spent a lot of time and became good friend with many poets and cultural personalities. Bashô continued to study *haikai*-poetry and several of his *hokku* were selected for publication in various anthologies. In 1672 he took the initiative to edit an anthology himself and managed to collect poems from some 30 poets. 1672 was also the year he left for Edo, which was not only the place where the *shôgun* resided, but also a city that had begun to compete with Kyôto and Ôsaka as the intellectual and cultural centre of Japan. Bashô received more and more assignments as judge in various *haikai*-competitions and in 1680 a collection called *Tôsei montei dokugin nijikkasen* (桃青門弟独吟二十歌仙), '20 independent *kasen* by Tôsei's disciples', was published – Tôsei (桃青) being the pseudonym used by Bashô at the time. Bashô was now so popular that his disciples built a house for him by the banks of the river Sumida. In the garden they planted a Japanese banana-plant, a *bashô*, which does not produce bananas, but has large, brittle leaves that easily break if there is a strong wind. He liked the plant so much that he changed his pseudonym to Bashô.

In 1684 Bashô undertook his first long journey, which was documented in *Nozarashi kikô* (野ざらし紀行), 'A weather-beaten journey', published in 1687. He was accompanied by one of his disciples, Kasuya Chiri (粕屋千里, 1648–1716) and the journey included a visit to his home-village, where his elder brother showed him a tress belonging to his mother who had died one year earlier. Bashô wrote:

> I arrived at my home-village during the ninth month. The grass was covered by frost and no traces (of her) were left. Everything had changed. My elder brother, with his white hair on the sides and wrinkles around his eyebrows, could only point out that we were still alive. Then he opened a memory-sack and said: 'Pay respect to your mother's white hair!' [...] We cried.

Bashô added:

> If I took it in my hand
> it would disappear in my warm tears
> autumn frost
> *Te ni toraba kien namida zo atsuki aki no shimo*[306]

Bashô was a sensitive poet whose values were firmly founded in Buddhist, Confucian, and Daoist thought. Bashô, although having seriously studied Zen, was never a monk belonging to a monastery, but he often dressed as priest and often stayed at temples and shrines. His great knowledge about, and interest in, the classical Nô theatre could also be seen as a reconfirmation of his religious beliefs. In Nô plays the story often centres around wandering priests and their encounters with spirits and demons. Nô did not have a clear educational purpose, but the moral in the plays had obvious Buddhist undertones.

Bashô, like many Japanese poets before him, was greatly influenced by classical Chinese poets, not least the well-known Tang dynasty poets Li Bai (李白, 701–762) and Du Fu (杜甫, 712–770), whom he admired immensely. In classical Chinese poetry there were certain ideals that were seen as necessary for a poet to embrace. One was the need to downplay one's own importance. Another was the poet's difficulties in agreeing with the perceived vulgarities of the societies in which the poets lived. And a third was the readiness to leave society whenever the poet felt it was necessary and wander around, seeking contact with masters of poetry and/or asceticism. These ideals were clearly a factor behind

306 Sugiura & Miyamoto & Ogino 1979:38.

the many travels on foot through Japan that Bashô undertook. *Nozarashi kikô* begins with the statement:

> I began a journey of 1000 *ri*,[307] without any provisions. I held on to the staff of an ancient, who is said to have entered nothingness under the midnight-moon. It was the eighth month of the first year of the Jôkyô reign[308] as I left my dilapidated hut by the river. The sound of the wind was oddly cold.[309]

The description says a lot about the ideals that Bashô honoured. The first poem of the journal is this one:

> Weather-beaten
> the wind pierces my body
> and soul
> *Nozarashi wo kokoro ni kaze no shimu mi kana*[310]

It is followed by:

> After ten autumns
> it is rather Edo
> which is my domicile
> *Aki totose kaette edo wo sasu kokyô*[311]

Bashô had actually lived in Edo for 13 years when he departed on this journey, but here he alludes to the Chinese poet Jia Dao (賈嶋, 779–843), who in a poem called 'Crossing the river Sang Gan' (渡桑乾) used the expression "10 autumns" as an expression indicating that a long time has passed.[312]

The harsh conditions for certain segments of society became painfully obvious to Bashô as he on this journey encountered an abandoned child, not more than two years old, along the Fuji river. The child was weeping in such a way that Bashô was convinced that his parents had left him in this "floating world", as treacherous as the rapids. The child seemed like a bush-clover

---

307 1 *ri* (里) is 2,44 miles. "1000" can here be read as "very long".
308 1684 CE.
309 Sugiura & Miyamoto & Ogino 1979:36.
310 Sugiura & Miyamoto & Ogino 1979.
311 Sugiura & Miyamoto & Ogino 1979.
312 Vargö 2018:132.

in the autumn-wind and Bashô threw him some food as he went on. The poem which followed is one of Bashô's most famous:

> You who listen to monkeys
> what about an abandoned child
> in the autumn-wind?
> *Saru wo kiku hito sutego ni aki no kaze ika ni*[313]

The cries of the monkeys in combination with the autumn-wind was often used in Chinese poetry to create an atmosphere of melancholy.

As Bashô continued to describe his journey, he referred to the Chinese poet Du Mu (杜牧, 803–853), saying:

> The moon could only be seen vaguely and at the base of the mountains it was still dark. I let my whip hanging and rode several *ri* on my horse before the rooster called. I thought of Du Mu's poem 'Early Departure' when suddenly my thoughts were scattered as we arrived at Sayo no Nakayama.[314]

Du Mu had written in his poem:

> I keep my whip hanging
> and trust the way my horse walks
> for several *li* no rooster can be heard
> we move through a grove
> still half dreaming
> when the leaves suddenly fall over me[315]

What then follows is a good description of how Bashô travelled and of his relationship to the religious world. He arrived at a Shintô shrine to worship and noted:

> I wear no sword at my belt, I carry an alms-bag hanging over my neck, and I hold a rosary with 18 beads in my hand. I look like a priest and my head is shaven, but I am a layman. Although I am not a priest, those with shaven heads are treated as Buddhists and are not allowed to enter the shrine.[316]

---

[313] Sugiura & Miyamoto & Ogino 1979:36.
[314] Vargö 2018:135.
[315] *li* is the same as *ri* in Japanese.
[316] Sugiura & Miyamoto & Ogino 1979:37–38.

Bashô was a Buddhist, but he was also a Shintôist, a Confucian, and a Daoist. He had studied Zen, but had enough attachments to this world to make him not want to enter a monastery, apart from short visits. He believed in anything and everything, treated religions with utmost respect, and yet he harbored enough doubts about the religious world to want to maintain his analytical freedom. He was primarily a poet, attracted to the ideal of classical poets, but he also enjoyed the life of a vagabond.

II

Later in his journal, Bashô composed a poem which shows his fondness for the daily life of local people and the poetic associations they give. He arrived at a scene where peasants were cleaning rice by using a *watayumi*, 'cotton bow', a bow which has a tendon attached to it. The sound created when someone hits the rice-covered ground with the cotton bow reminded Bashô of the sound of the *biwa*-lute:

> A *watayumi*
> the soothing sound of a *biwa*
> behind the bamboo
> *Watayumi ya biwa ni nagusamu take no oku*[317]

Bashô and Kasuya Chiri then continued their journey on foot to the Buddhist temple Futagamiyama Taima, where there is an enormous pine-tree in the garden. The tree is probably over 1000 years old and has grown so large that an ox can hide behind it. Bashô was happy that people had not been tempted to cut it down. He wrote that although the tree is not a living creature, "its relationship to Buddha has preserved it from the sin of the axe".[318] The poem which followed also alluded to Chinese saints, in this case the Chinese philosopher Zhuangzi (莊子, said to have lived 370–287 BCE), who wrote about a giant tree that could hide a thousand cows.

> Monks and morning-glories
> how many incarnations

[317] Sugiura & Miyamoto & Ogino 1979:39.
[318] Sugiura & Miyamoto & Ogino 1979.

at this *dharma*-pine?
Sô asagao iku shinikaeru nori no matsu[319]

Bashô was later joined by a monk from the Izu province, who had heard that the great *hokku*-master was wandering in the vicinity:

Now together
we can eat ears of barley
on our wandering
Iza tomo ni ho mugi kurawan kusamakura[320]

While on the road, Bashô was reached by the sad news that Daiten (大顛, 1629–1685), the abbot of the well-known Zen temple in Kamakura, Engakuji, had passed away. Daiten was a priest and poet, who often composed linked poetry together with Takarai Kikaku (宝井其角, 1661–1707), one of Bashô's most important disciples. Bashô wrote a letter to Kikaku expressing his sorrow and lamenting the fact that it had taken so long for him to get the news. The apricot-flowers had already bloomed so Bashô prayed for the soul of the abbot in front of some hydrangeas (hortensias) instead, letting the missing apricot-flowers symbolize the deceased:

I miss the apricot-flowers
and pray in front of hydrangeas
in tears
Ume koite u no hana ogamu namida kana[321]

The first paragraph in one of his next travel-journals, *Kashima Kikô* (鹿島紀行, 1687), is a good illustration of the conditions under which poets and monks travelled. Bashô was determined to see the moon over the mountains at the Kashima-shrine in autumn and was accompanied by two men: one a masterless samurai, who also wrote poetry, the other an itinerant monk. The monk wore black robes, reminding Bashô of a crow, and a pouch for sacred objects hanging around his neck. In a portable shrine, which the monk carried on his back, there was an image of the Buddha. As

[319] Sugiura & Miyamoto & Ogino 1979.
[320] Sugiura & Miyamoto & Ogino 1979:43. The word *kusamakura* means 'grass pillow' and is a metaphor for wandering.
[321] Sugiura & Miyamoto & Ogino 1979.

for himself Bashô said he was neither a monk, nor a man of the world. He likened himself to a bat, something in-between a bird and a mouse.

As they continued their pilgrimage they arrived at a place called Fusa, near the Tone river. It was a place where fishermen use to catch salmon. They boarded a boat and crossed the river to Kashima, where the Zen priest, who had been Bashô's teacher, served as abbot in a temple. They were invited to spend the night there. It had been raining during the night, but in the early dawn the sky cleared somewhat and Bashô woke everyone. The light of the moon in combination with the sound of the rain was almost a religious experience, but Bashô was disappointed that he could not see the full moon. Swiftly moving clouds kept interfering with the scene; it looked in fact as if the moon itself was moving quickly:

> The moon moves quickly
> as the tree-tops keep
> holding the rain
> *Tsuki hayashi kozue wa ame wo mochinagara*

In 1687 Bashô also published his *Oi no kobumi*, 'Notes from my travel-knapsack'.[322] The first paragraphs sum up Bashô's philosophy quite well:

> Among the hundreds of bones and nine openings of the human body there is something, a spirit of mine, which one can temporarily call 'Monk blowing in the wind'. It is thin and can easily be torn to pieces. For long it has been fond of wild verses, which has become a vice for life. Sometimes it has been full of despair and tried to put the verses aside, sometimes it has felt an exaggerated pride of having reached sublime levels. It has always been indecisive and too eager. At one point it tried to calm itself through worldly success, but poetry put an end to that. On another occasion it tried to enlighten itself through scholastic studies, but also at that time wild verses came in-between as an obstacle. In the end it realized that poetry was the only way to continue. Saigyô's *waka*-poetry,

[322] The character *oi* (笈) was a box made of bamboo carried like a knapsack. It was often used by itinerant priests or wandering monks for their few possessions, not least scriptures, books or notebooks.

Sôgi's linked verses, Sesshû's painting, Rikyu's tea-ceremony – they all have something in common: that which is artfully refined. [...] Those who do not see the flowers are like barbarians. Those who do not leave room for flowers in their hearts are like animals. By leaving barbarism and distancing oneself from the animals one can become part of nature. It was the beginning of the month when the gods were absent.[323] The skies were unsettled and as for myself, I was an autumn-leaf in the wind, not knowing where to go.[324]

Wanderer
will I call myself
the first winter-rain
Tabibito to waga na yobaren hatsu shigure

A poet, who called himself Chôtarô and followed Bashô a bit on his journey, added the following verse:

And the camellias
will serve as your
lodgings
Mata sazanka wo yadoyado ni shite[325]

Bashô's most famous travel account is also a record of his longest trip on foot: *Oku no hosomichi*, 'The narrow roads to the inner parts (of the country)'. It was a trip that lasted 150 days. His travel companion for the main part of the journey was the disciple Sora (曽良, 1649–1710), who wrote his own diary about the experience. Before leaving they took an emotional farewell of their friends, who had followed them across the river Sumida. It was the 27th of March according to the moon-calendar, and the 16th of May according to the modern one.

Passing spring
the birds cry and fish
have tears in their eyes
Yuku haru ya tori naku uo no me wa namida[326]

---

323 October according to the moon-calendar.
324 Sugiura & Miyamoto & Ogino 1979:52.
325 Sugiura & Miyamoto & Ogino 1979.
326 Sugiura & Miyamoto & Ogino 1979:71.

There are many references to Buddhist temples and legends in *Oku no hosomichi* and the purpose of the trip was not only to "be one with nature" and write poetry, but also to visit famous religious sites. Having wandered a long distance for several days, Bashô and Sora reached the Buddhist temple Risshaku in Yamagata, belonging to the esoteric Tendai sect. The temple is also called Yamadera, 'the mountain temple', as it is situated on the top of a mountain. The many steps leading up to the temple were exhausting to climb and the summer heat was intense. The cicadas were crying loudly and broke the silence.

Stillness,
the cry of the cicadas
penetrates the rock
Shizukasa ya iwa ni shimi-iru semi no koe[327]

Towards the end of this long journey Bashô was staying overnight at a Zen temple belonging to the Sôtô-sect, Zenshôji. It was customary for guests to sweep the temple-garden as a form of payment before leaving. When Bashô began to use the broom, a couple of monks came running with paper, brush, and ink, asking him to write a poem for them:

Sweeping the garden
before leaving the temple
as willow-leaves fall
Niwa haite idebaya tera ni chiru yanagi[328]

Bashô continued to the temple Tenryûji, also belonging to the Sôtô sect. He knew the abbot there well. This time Bashô was followed on his way to the temple by a person who called himself Hokushi, 'Northern Branch' (北枝). Hokushi also wanted to receive a poem. Bashô tore off a piece of a folding-fan and wrote:

I write something
and tear off a piece of the fan
as memory
Mono kaite ôgi hikisaku nagori kana[329]

---

[327] Sugiura & Miyamoto & Ogino 1979:87.
[328] Sugiura & Miyamoto & Ogino 1979:95.
[329] Sugiura & Miyamoto & Ogino 1979:96.

III

Bashô approached the end of this journey, but first arrived at the famous Zen temple Eiheiji, established by the founder of the Sôtô sect, the Zen master Dôgen (道元禅師, 1200–1253), where he wanted to pray before moving on to Higuchi castle, where he heard the first wild geese of autumn. The moon was exceptionally bright in the evening, when he came to an inn and asked the inn-keeper if it would be as bright the next evening. The innkeeper told him that it was impossible to tell and offered him some *sake*. Bashô also wanted to take the opportunity to worship at the site of emperor Chûai,[330] where "the moon-light filtered through pines and white sands spread before the sanctuary like frost".[331] The inn-keeper told Bashô that a priest called Taa Shônin (他阿上人, 1237–1319) wanted worshippers to be able to come to the site without problems and therefore cut the grass and brought lots of sand and stones to cover the muddy ground. Taa Shônin was the second abbot at the temple Yugyôji (遊行寺), 'Temple of Pilgrims' – the first one being Ippen Shônin (一遍上人, 1239–1289), an itinerant priest who founded the Jishû, 'Time sect' (時宗), a branch of the Pure Land sect, Jôdoshû (浄土宗). Inspired by Taa Shônin, priests have continued to bring sand to the site in a yearly ceremony called *sunamochi*, 'bringing sand'.

> The clear moon
> over the pilgrims
> bringing sand
> *Tsuki kiyoshi yugyô no moteru suna no ue*[332]

Bashô died relatively young, only 50 years old, and although this was a respected age in his time he could have lived much longer had he taken better care of himself. He died on his way to Ôsaka. Bashô had been invited to attend several poetry-sessions and forced himself to accept the invitations in spite of feeling ill. A few days before the end he wrote the following poem:

> This autumn
> why do I age this way?

---

330 仲哀天皇, the 14th emperor of Japan, died 200 CE.

331 Barnhill 2005:75.

332 Sugiura & Miyamoto & Ogino 1979:97; Barnhill 2005:75–76; Vargö 2018:364.

A bird flies into a cloud
Kono aki wa nande toshi yoru kumo ni tori[333]

Finally, Bashô had to decline an invitation to attend a poetry-session, because of his illness, but from the house where he was resting, he sent a poem, filled with dry humour, to the host. He was lying in bed and wondering what the noise coming from a neighbour was all about:

The autumn is deep
the person next door
what is he up to?
Aki fukaki tonari wa nani wo suru hito zo[334]

Three days before he died Bashô wrote his farewell-poem:

Fallen ill on the journey
my dreams wander around
the withered field
Tabi ni yande yume wa kareno wo kakemeguru[335]

Bashô was a wandering poet, religious at times, less religious on other occasions. On his journeys he dressed as a Buddhist priest, partly because he wanted to travel like an itinerant priest, partly because it gave him protection against robbers, since priests were not known for carrying anything valuable. Through his travel-journals Bashô created an ideal world of itinerant monks and is often hailed as a role-model for wandering religious poets. Today one can find large stones with inscriptions of his poems along the routes he took.

References

Barnhill, David L. 2005. *Bashô's Journey: The Literary Prose of Matsuo Bashô*. New York: State University of New York Press.

Sugiura & Miyamoto & Ogino. 1979 (1959). *Bashô bunshû*. Nihon koten bungaku taikei 46. Iwanami Shoten.

Vargö, Lars. 2018. *Bashô: Blommornas, fåglarnas och månens poet*. Carlsson bokförlag.

[333] Vargö 2018:576.
[334] Vargö 2018:578.
[335] Vargö 2018:578–579.

Author Presentations

Kristoffer af Edholm is PhD Student in History of Religions at Stockholm University and has studied Indo-European religions, Vedic ritual, ancient Indian kingship, asceticism, and renunciation. Among his publications we find: "Royal Splendour in the Waters: Vedic Śrī- and Avestan X^{v}arənah-" (*Indo-Iranian Journal* 60, 2017). [ORCID: https://orcid.org/0000-0002-5786-1421]

Peter Jackson Rova is Professor in History of Religions at Stockholm University, specializing in the study of Indo-European religions, with particular emphasis on ancient India and Iran, Mediterranean Antiquity, and the pagan Germanic world. Among his publications is the co-edited volume *Philosophy and the End of Sacrifice: Disengaging Ritual in Ancient India and Beyond* (Equinox 2015). [ORCID: https://orcid.org/000-002-0742-6640]

Per Kværne was Professor in History of Religions at the University of Oslo from 1975 until 2012, and has been Visiting Professor at the University of Oxford and at École Pratique des Hautes Études in Paris. Among his published works is: *An Anthology of Buddhist Tantric Songs: A Study of the Caryāgīti* (Universitetsforlaget 1977, White Orchid Press 1986, Orchid Press 2010).

Stefan Larsson is Research Fellow and Senior Lecturer at the University of Gävle. He received his PhD in History of Religions from Stockholm University in 2009. Larsson's research focuses on the non-monastic and practice-oriented aspects of Tibetan Buddhism, particularly as evidenced in Buddhist songs and biographical literature. His publications include: *Crazy for Wisdom: The Making of a Mad Yogin in Fifteenth-Century Tibet* (Brill 2012). [ORCID: https://orcid.org/0000-0002-1320-7073]

Lars Vargö was Ambassador of Sweden in South Korea 2006–2011 and in Japan 2011–2014. He earned his PhD in Japanese Studies in 1982. Among Vargö's recent books we find *Bashô: Blommornas, fåglarnas och månens poet*, which is a complete translation of the poems of Matsuo Bashô into Swedish (Carlsson 2018).

Heinz Werner Wessler is Professor in Indology at Uppsala University. He has published on classical Hinduism, Sikhism, and modern and contemporary literature, for example: "The Grammar of Assi: Kashinath Singh and Globalizing Banaras", in Keul (ed.), *Revisiting Benares: Scholarly Pilgrimages to the City of Light* (Harrassowitz 2014).

www.ingramcontent.com/pod-product-compliance
Ingram Content Group UK Ltd.
Pitfield, Milton Keynes, MK11 3LW, UK
UKHW022003190726
13853UKWH00004B/1706